Gymnasium Spaichingen

Lernmittel Nr.: ~~E7~~ E6 / 105

	Name, Vorname	Klasse	Schuljahr
1.	Winker Simone	11d	05/06
2.	Brecht Uta	10a	06/07
3.	Sarah Burke	11d	07/08
4.	Annika Furrer	10a	08/09
5.	Kevin Schmieder	11c	09/10
6.			

D1730634

Pathway to Summit

Oberstufe Englisch

Herausgegeben von: James Martin

Mitarbeiter: Susan Ashworth-Fiedler, Veronika Kaiser, James Martin, Angelika Rösner

Sprachliche Betreuung: James Martin

Best.-Nr. 040030 6

Umschlagentwurf: Hans-Georg Grassl

Website: www.schoeningh.de

E-Mail: info@schoeningh.de

© 1999 Ferdinand Schöningh, Paderborn;
ab 2002 Schöningh Verlag im Westermann Schulbuchverlag GmbH,
Jühenplatz 1–3, D-33098 Paderborn

Alle Rechte vorbehalten. Dieses Werk sowie einzelne Teile desselben sind urheberrechtlich geschützt. Jede Verwertung in anderen als den gesetzlich zugelassenen Fällen ist ohne vorherige schriftliche Zustimmung des Verlages nicht zulässig.

Druck: westermann druck GmbH, Braunschweig

Druck   6   5   4   Jahr   06   05   04

ISBN 3-14-040030-6

Alle deutschsprachigen Teile dieses Werkes folgen der reformierten Rechtschreibung und Zeichensetzung.

Contents

	Vorwort	5
	Abbreviations	6
Literature:	• How To Eat A Poem by Eve Merriam	8
Getting Behind	• Haiku	9
The Lines	• Wedding Night by Tom Hawkins	10
	• Hunger by Barker Fairley	12
	• Arnie's Test Day by Barry Peters	13
	• Coat by Vicki Feaver	16
	• Twelve Songs (IX) by Wystan Hugh Auden	17
	• Discovery Of A Father by Sherwood Anderson	18
	• One Art by Elizabeth Bishop	23
	• The Tiny Closet by William Inge	25
	• The Rose by Amanda McBroom	32

The South: **A Unique History**
More Than Just
A Region

What Is So Different About The South? Five People, Five Different Answers	35
• The Primitive by Don L. Lee	37
The Road From Slavery To Freedom	38
• Childhood In The Slave Quarters by Booker T. Washington	39

The Civil War

From Plantation Life To Civil War	42
The Spy's A Broad	43
Reconstruction: Rebuilding The South	45

Civil Rights

From Freedom To Civil Rights	47
Martin Luther King Jr: The Man And His Message	50
Black Migration From The South 1940–1970	51
• Going Back Home by Son Seals	51
• You Stand Accused Of Being Black by Mildred D. Taylor	52

A Taste Of The South

Ol' Man River Tells His Tale	54
River Riddles	56
• Singing These Old Lonesome Blues by Julius Lester	57
Jazz And Jazzmen	58
Iced Tea: The Champagne Of The South	60

The Southwest:
Home To Many
Cultures

Endless Horizons	62
The People Of The Southwest: Their Past And Present	63
Exploring The Navajo Nation	65
Visit To A Navajo Park	67
• Without Title by Diane Glancy	69
The Mexican-American Border: A Golden Door?	70
Hot On The Trail	71
Along The Rio Grande	73
So Long 'Dallas,' Hello High Tech	74

Contents

Great Britain: Regional Perspectives

"Rich South, Poor North" Tell That To The Cornish 78
The Millennium Dome 79
Britain's Cities Are Booming 82
Business Success 84
Scotland's Cultural Cocktail 85
A Vision Of The Highlands 88
• Pride Of Lions by Geddes Thomson 89
Hometown 92

Devolution In Great Britain

Devolution? That's A Pop Group, Isn't It? 94
Decisive Vote By Scots 95
The Welsh Decision 97
A United Kingdom? 98

Great Britain And Europe: Merry Old England And Brave New Europe

English Is The Most Commonly Taught Language In Europe 102
The Madness Of Metrication 103
• Measure For Measure by Margaret Walker 104
Britain And Europe 105
Farmers Philosophical Over Latest Blow 107
British Farmers Demonstrate Against EU Policies 108
Would It Have Been Better If We Hadn't Joined The EU? .. 109
Selling The Euro To The British 112
A Modern Britain, With America And In Europe 114
Hilaire Belloc's View 115
Cartoonists' Views 116
An Interview With Britain's Prime Minister 117
Education And Training: Tackling Unemployment In The
   European Job Market 119
Newspapers On The Internet 121

Our Environment: Don't Destroy It; Save It!

Global Warming: The First Victims 123
Endangered Creatures 124
An Ocean Of Concern 126
The Tracks We Left Behind Weren't Ours 127
Looking Forward To The Ride 128
Energy-Saving Tips For The Home 130
Dirty Harry 131
Respect The Land 132

Acknowledgements 135

Vorwort

Pathway to Summit ist das Lehrbuch zur Einführung in die Oberstufenarbeit und bildet eine konzeptionelle Einheit mit dem weiterführenden Lehrwerk **Summit**.

Es bietet eine Vielzahl authentischer britischer und amerikanischer Texte, die eine lehrplangerechte Einführung in die Landeskunde und Literatur der beiden Sprachbereiche leisten.

Bei der Textauswahl wurde darauf geachtet, dass die einzelnen Kapitel durch unterschiedliche Textsorten möglichst abwechslungsreich gestaltet sind. Dadurch erfahren Schüler die englische Sprache in ihrer ganzen Vielfalt vom Gedicht über das Interview bis hin zu Texten aus aktuellen Tageszeitungen. Zur schnellen Orientierung sind fiktionale Texte im Inhaltsverzeichnis mit einem grünen Punkt versehen. Besonderer Wert wurde darauf gelegt, dass die Texte sowohl in ihrem Umfang wie auch in ihrer Thematik schülergerecht sind.

Aktuelle Sachtexte wurden auf ihren exemplarischen Charakter und ihre allgemeine Gültigkeit hin überprüft. Ihre unterschiedlichen Schwierigkeitsgrade ermöglichen eine Differenzierung schulischer Anforderungen.

Einen besonderen Service bietet dieser Band dadurch, dass viele Texte mit ausgesuchten Adressen zu weiteren sich im Internet befindlichen Informationen *(websites)* versehen sind. Damit wird sowohl die Aktualität der Informationen unterstützt als auch der Umgang mit dem neuesten Kommunikationsmedium im Unterricht angeregt.

Da die Literatur in der Oberstufe einen wichtigen Stellenwert einnimmt, wurde diesem Kapitel der ihm gebührende Platz am Anfang des Buches eingeräumt. Es enthält Beispiele verschiedenster literarischer Gattungen, sogar ein vollständiges Kurzdrama.

Um vor der Konfrontation mit den Sachtexten das Vorwissen der Schüler zu bestimmten Themenbereichen zu reaktivieren, gibt es am Anfang jedes Kapitels eine „*Getting to know …*"-Aufgabe. Ebenso sind vielen der einzelnen Texte eine „*pre-reading activity*", ein visueller Impuls (Bilder, Fotos, Zeichnungen, Collagen, usw.) oder eine kurze Einführung vorangestellt. Dadurch werden die Erwartungen und das Interesse der Schülerinnen und Schüler geweckt, die Texterschließung wird erleichtert.

Die jedem Text folgenden Aufgabenapparate bieten Fragen zum Inhalt des Textes *(understanding, analysing, discussing the text)* sowie Anregungen zum produktiven Umgang mit dem neuen Wissen *(going beyond the text, creative writing)*. Zur Erweiterung des Sprachhorizonts der Schüler befinden sich nach den Texten auch zahlreiche „*translation-*" und „*language-*"Aufgaben.

Als weitere Hilfe stehen am Ende jedes der landeskundlichen Kapitel Aufgaben zur Arbeit mit dem neu erworbenen thematischen Wortschatz. Im Literaturkapitel helfen den Schülern die Informationskästchen zur Erschließung des literarischen Vokabulars, das für die Textarbeit in der Oberstufe wichtig ist.

Die kontextbezogenen Worterklärungen sind so gestaltet, dass die Schüler den Text spontan verstehen können. Die vielen Angaben der Lautschrift ermöglichen einen bei mündlichen Äußerungen flüssigeren Umgang mit dem Text.

Wir wünschen Schülerinnen und Schülern wie Lehrerinnen und Lehrern eine erfolgreiche Arbeit mit **Pathway to Summit**.

Abbreviations

abbr	abbreviation	l, ll	line, lines
adj	adjective	Mex	Mexican-Spanish
arch	archaic	n	noun
Brit	British usage or pronunciation	orig	originally
cf	confer, compare	p, pp	page, pages
derog	derogatory	pl	plural
eg	exempli gratia; for example	pp	past participle
esp	especially	pt	past tense
etc	et cetera; and so on	rhet	rhetorical
euph	euphemistic	sb	somebody
fig	figurative	Scot	Scottish
idm	idiom	sl	slang
fml	formal	sth	something
idm	idiom	US	American usage or pronunciation
ie	id est, that is	usu	usually
infml	informal		

The phonetic transcriptions in the annotations are taken from the *Oxford Advanced Learner's Dictionary,* Fifth Edition, (Oxford University Press, 1995).

Texts marked with an asterisk denote those written by an author of *Pathway to Summit.*

Literature:
Getting Behind The Lines

 Literature

Getting to know your attitude towards literature
- What kind of texts do you read in your spare time?
- Why do you think people read?
- Why do you think people write?
- Have you ever written a story or a poem yourself?
- How does poetry differ from prose?

How To Eat A Poem

Don't be polite.
Bite in.
Pick it up with your fingers and lick the juice that
    may run down your chin.
5 It is ready and ripe now, whenever you are.

You do not need a knife or fork or spoon
or plate or napkin or tablecloth.
For there is no core
or stem
10 or rind
or pit
or seed
or skin
to throw away.

Eve Merriam

Analysing the poem
1. What does Eve Merriam compare a poem with?
2. What does the speaker recommend doing with a poem?
3. What information are we given in this poem about the relationship between the reader and the poem?

Getting a taste for other poems
Find all the poems in *Pathway to Summit*. Which ones did you read to the end and why?

> The **speaker** is not always identical to the poet but is often a different persona with certain feelings or attitudes that are conveyed within the poem. The speaker is therefore a part of the structure of a poem, as well as a vehicle for expressing meaning.
>
> A **line** is a row of words on a page.

---

3 to lick to touch your lips with your tongue **4 chin** part of the face below your mouth **7 napkin** serviette **8 core** central part of sth **9 stem** part of a plant from which the leaves grow **10 rind** [raɪnd] hard outer skin **11 pit** (esp US) = Brit stone **12 seed** part of a plant that will grow into a new one

Getting Behind The Lines

Haiku

Haiku is a form
of Japanese poetry
that shows an image.

Haiku have three lines:
5 one with seven syllables
and two have five each.

A haiku appeals
directly to our senses
through its images.

10 Haiku give you one
moment of intense insight,
state a clear picture.

A haiku uses
images drawn from nature,
15 reveals a season.

Forget metaphors!
Rhyme is not necessary!
sentences can be [incomplete]

Simplicity and
20 directness of the haiku
make them attractive.

one observation -
impersonal description -
spoken in one breath

25 Read these three haiku:
point out each one's images,
senses, the season.*

On an old oak tree
the last leaf of autumn hangs,
waiting to be free.
Anonymous

The heavy winter snows
have capped with white the pine-tree tops
where sleep the big black crows.
Anonymous

old pond...
a frog leaps in
water's sound
Matsuo Bashō

Creative writing

1. Write your own *haiku*.
   Share them with other pupils.
   Enjoy the process.

2. Write *haiku* in groups.
   Add a second to the first.
   Keep to one subject.

   Collaboration
   results in surprising thoughts.
   Words create insights.

An **image** is an imaginative description or comparison that produces a picture in the mind of the reader or listener.

---

5 syllable ['sɪləbl] *Silbe* **7 to appeal** to to be attractive to, interesting for **11 insight** understanding, esp sudden, of the true nature of sth **15 to reveal** to cause or allow sth to be seen
to cap to cover the top or end of sth **pond** *Teich*

 Literature

Wedding Night
Tom Hawkins

I have worked at this bus station magazine stand since nineteen fifty three, waiting for the right girl to come along. When I took this job, the paint on that wall over there was new, it was a light green color then. The servicemen from the Korean War would stop and buy cigarettes, and I learned the insignia from the Army, Coast Guard, Navy, and Marines.

Once I was held up by a stocky white man in a brown jacket. Showed me the two teeth he had left in his head and the barrel of a little tape-wrapped automatic pointed at my heart. I gave him all the dough but never felt scared. Way I saw it, he was just like me, and I could die behind that counter and just walk away inside his skin, with a few dollars to spend. We were all one thing. So I handed him the money, feeling richer right away – three hundred twenty-three dollars – and let him get away before I called the cops.

I heard they never caught him, then I heard they caught him in another state – Utah I think – and then I heard they found him dead in an airport parking lot in Kansas. I don't know. He may be out there yet. He may be back. May hold me up tonight, or just shoot me dead, or both.

Anything can happen in the bus station. In the nineteen-sixties, we had what we called the hippies, young people in ragged get-ups. They used to sleep all over the furniture in sleeping bags, with packs and rolled-up tents.

That's when I began to think that the right girl might come along after all, some girl who'd grown tired of the long-haired boys, and tired of the road, and walk home with me and hold my hand, and curl up with me in my bed and on my squeaky springs. I kept an eye out. One day I saw a young lady: she looked so long-tired and in need of a friend. I bought her a sandwich and coffee and a peanut-butter cup. I bought her some aspirin and a pint of milk, fingernail clippers and a souvenir shirt.

I told her I had a place where she could come to rest and stay, as long as she might want. I told her it wasn't fancy and wasn't but one room, but what was mine was hers. I knew it was clean. I'd cleaned it up the day before when I saw this girl hanging around.

She stroked my hair and said my heart was full of love. She said she had to sleep about twelve hours and then she'd go away. I took her home. She slumped down on the bed and cried – told me I was "so very kind." And then she slept like the dead. I lay down on the floor beside her, where I said I'd stay. In the middle of the night I woke up on fire, and the room was turning. I couldn't think. The air turned furry, where I crept up and slid in bed beside her, that girl still completely dressed. She breathed like the sea. I touched her skin, just her skin inside her clothes. She really never woke, just sighed and turned. In the morning when I woke up in the bed, she was gone.

I've worked here since nineteen fifty three, waiting for the right girl to come along. I guess she did. Some good marriages don't last long.

---

5 serviceman soldier **6 Korean War** (1950–53) war between the UN forces (primarily the US and South Korea) and North Korea **7 insignia** [ɪnˈsɪɡnɪə] sign that shows sb is a member of a military regiment **8 Marine** [məˈriːn] soldier trained to serve on land or sea **9 to hold up** here: to rob **stocky** short, strong and solid in appearance **11 barrel** Lauf **12 automatic** here: pistol **13 dough** [dəʊ] (sl) money; *"Knete"* **15 counter** long, flat surface over which goods are sold in a shop **25 yet** *noch* **29 ragged** [ˈræɡɪd] (of clothes) old and torn **get-up** (infml) here: clothes **31 pack** here: backpack **37 spring** here: *Feder* **40 peanut-butter cup** type of sweets combining peanut-butter and milk chocolate **41 pint** [paɪnt] 0.47 of a litre in the US; 0.57 of a litre in Britain **41/42 clipper** instrument used to cut sth **49 to stroke** act of passing one's hand gently over sth several times **52 to slump down** here: *fallen lassen* **57 furry** *pelzartig*

Getting Behind The Lines

Understanding the text	Retell in your own words what happens in the story.
Analysing the text	Compare the parallel elements in the two parts of the story: the hold up in the magazine stand and the coming and going of the tired girl. Complete the following chart.

1. bus station magazine stand	1. one room
2. the paint on the wall was new	2. it was clean
3. Korean War	3. Vietnam War
4. insignia of the soldiers' uniforms	4.
5. servicemen (with crew cuts)	etc.
6. he was held up	.
etc.	.

Discussing the text	1. How do you think the man would define marriage? 2. Discuss the title.
Going beyond the text	Write a description of the main character as you imagine him: age, hobbies, appearance, etc. Back up your description as much as possible with words from the text.
Creative writing	Write about one of the two main incidents from another point of view. For example, write about the robbery from the robber's point of view or about the "wedding night" from the girl's point of view.
Translate	Lines 32–39. Choose your words as carefully as the author did.

The **narrator** is the person who tells the story. The narrator may be a character involved in the story or a persona whose role is to simply tell the story as an observer. The narrator as a character within the story narrates events as he/she sees them and interprets other characters' actions as they affect him/her. A story narrated by such a narrator may therefore be personal or intimate, although at the same time it can limit the reader's knowledge of other characters.
The narrator as an independent observer knows all the characters equally well and may therefore present a more balanced and objective account of events.
Point of view is the literary term used to describe the position from which the narrator sees and presents the action and characters.
A **first-person point of view** is marked by the use of "I" and usually displays great detail about the narrator's feelings and thoughts. When talking about the speaker, we call him/her the **first-person narrator.**
A narrator-character may also sometimes narrate from a **third-person point of view,** although this is more commonly found with the narrator-observer. The third-person point of view may be **limited,** i.e. knowing only a few characters' feelings and thoughts, or it may be **omniscient** [ɒmˈnɪsɪənt], i.e. knowing everything. When an author wishes to present the view of a particular person or type of person, this is known as **perspective;** for example, a story told from the perspective of a child, a movie star, or a poor farmer, etc.

Literature

Hunger

Hungry I was
and fed on fullness,
yet life was such
I knew but dullness.

5 Older I am
and yet am younger,
my life is full,
I feed on hunger.

Barker Fairley

Analysing the poem

1. The poem concentrates on the following 5 key words: hungry/to feed on/fullness/life/dullness. What is said in this poem can be illustrated with these key words in the following pattern which is called chiasmus (see box, p.13).

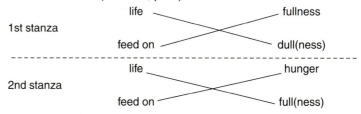

Verbalise these 2 patterns using a main clause and a subordinate clause with "although."

2. Create a third statement from the poem with a sentence starting with "although."

Going beyond the poem

1. What could the poetic "I" have been hungry for?
2. What might the poetic "I" be lacking now that he is older?
3. Why do you think the poetic "I" is still hungry?

2 to feed (pt, pp fed) **on sth** to eat **4 dullness** [dʌl] lack of excitement

Getting Behind The Lines

Chiasmus [kɪˈazməs] is a sequence of two phrases or clauses which are parallel in syntax, but with a reversal in the order of words.

Stanza refers to a group of lines in a poem, often with a regular pattern of **rhyme** and **rhythm**. A group of two lines in a poem, especially when they rhyme, is known as a **couplet,** while a group of three lines is a **triplet.**

When the first person singular occurs in a poem, another term, the **poetic** "I" (the lyrical "I"), is often used in place of the **speaker.** Like the **speaker,** the **poetic** "I" is not identical to the poet, but contributes to the poem's meaning and is a way for the poet to express certain ideas, thoughts and feelings.

Pre-reading activity How do you feel when you have several tests at school in one week?

Arnie's Test Day
Barry Peters

Arnie Watson, facing five tests on a spring Friday of his junior year at Riverdale High School, sat in his bedroom at five a.m. and wrote all over his clothes. Beneath the bill of his Chicago Bulls cap, Arnie wrote in Spanish twenty of the vocabulary words from a list that he was provided with by Señora Martin on Monday and told to memorize by Friday. Certainly Arnie would have memorized those words, just as he had done with vocabulary lists all year, had he not been on the phone for two hours Thursday night trying to convince Marilou Spencer not to break up with him. Dismayed when Marilou slammed the phone in his ear, Arnie couldn't concentrate on his Español the rest of the night. Exasperated, he rose early on Friday and meticulously wrote those twenty words and shorthand definitions in fine black ink on the underside of the cap's red bill.
Frankly, Arnie didn't have the chance to study history, either, that week. Gus Finley and Arnie were going to meet at the Riverdale Library on Tuesday and study the amendments to the Constitution, but Arnie got stuck in the house after a fight with his parents. How are you going to get into a real college, they yelled, a Michigan or a Duke or a Stanford, if you fall out of the top five percent

---

3 junior year (US) 11th grade **8 bill** (US) front of a cap that protects the eyes **21 to convince** to persuade sb to do sth **23 dismayed** (adj) shocked and discouraged **24 to slam** to put down with great force **27 exasperated** (adj) [-ˈ----] annoyed about sth that cannot be changed **28 meticulous** [-ˈ---] giving great care and attention and detail **29 shorthand** shorter and simpler way of expressing sth **32 frank** open, honest **37 amendment to the Constitution** change or addition to the US Constitution **38 to get stuck** not able to leave **41 to yell** to shout **41/42 Michigan, Duke, Stanford** names of some of the best American universities

Literature

of your class, if you bring home any more eighty percents in your honors classes? Just you wait and see, Arnie retorted, storming upstairs to his bedroom. It won't be possible, they said.
Knowing that he couldn't leave the house after such a scene, Arnie didn't meet Gus at the library, which is why on that Friday morning before school, Arnie wrote abbreviated versions of the amendments on the inside collar of his Reebok polo shirt, actually needing to write on the inside of the shirt itself, repealing Prohibition just above his heart.
Luck ran against Arnie that week in English, too. Mr. Phelan, the Riverdale basketball coach, told his players they had better be at spring conditioning OR ELSE. Naturally, Arnie wanted to stay on Phelan's good side for his senior season, so Arnie ran and lifted weights with the rest of the team after school that week, precluding him from reading all but the first chapter of *The Great Gatsby*. On Friday morning, then, Arnie wrote "Jay Gatsby" and "Nick Caraway" and "Tom Buchanan" and "Daisy Buchanan" on the tanned inside of his belt along with a very brief synopsis of their literal and metaphorical roles in the novel; on the pale blue inside waistband of his jeans, Arnie elaborated on Fitzgerald's symbolism, even drawing a pair of spectacles overlooking a map of East Egg and West Egg, Gatsby's mansion, a heap of ashes and a skyscraper representing New York City, praying that the information he had gleaned from *Cliff's Notes* would be useful on Mrs. Schenck's in-class essay.

Possibly the most difficult test for Arnie would be physics. Quantum theory was hard enough for Arnie to understand during lectures and labs; finding time to memorize formulas for Friday's test was another problem.
Right when he opened his notebook on Wednesday night, Arnie's grandmother called to say that Grampa had been admitted to Riverdale Hospital with chest pains. So Arnie and his parents spent three hours at the hospital, where Arnie read *People* magazine instead of *Introduction to Physics* while waiting for the doctors to report Grampa's condition. They said Grampa would have surgery on Friday – Arnie's test day – only a few hours after Arnie wrote quantum physics formulas on the outside of his polyester white socks.
Unusual as it was, Arnie faced a fifth test that Friday in trigonometry. Vindicating himself for being required to attend Riverdale Lutheran Church choir practice last night – after basketball conditioners and before his devastating phone call to Marilou Spencer, after lying to his parents that no, he did not have any tests on Friday, after answering countless questions from other choir members about his grandfather's impending heart operation – Arnie wrote trigonometry notes on the bottom white soles of his Air Jordan basketball shoes. Why me, Arnie thought, and next to the silhouette logo of Michael Jordan flying above the world,

---

44 eighty percents *Note befriedigend* **honors class** (Brit **honour**) similar to *Leistungskurs* **45 to retort** to make a quick reply to an accusation **51 abbreviated** shortened **52 collar** ['kɒlə(r)] part of clothing around the neck **54 to repeal** to abolish or cancel **55 Prohibition** period of time (1920–1933) during which a constitutional amendment made it illegal to produce or sell alcoholic drinks in the US **58 coach** *Trainer* **59 spring conditioning** (US) first training phase used to get athletes fit for the new season **60 to stay on sb's good side** *jdm wohlgesonnen sein* **61 senior** (US; adj) relating to the last year of school **63 to preclude sb from doing sth** to make sth impossible **67 tanned** here: *gegerbt* **68 brief** short **synopsis** [sɪˈnɒpsɪs] summary of a book or play **literal** concerned with the basic or usual meaning of sth **69 metaphorical** concerned with the imaginative use of sth **69/70 pale blue** opposite of dark blue **70 waistband** *Hosenbund* **70/71 to elaborate on sth** [ɪˈlæbəreɪt] to describe sth in detail **72 spectacles** [ˈspektəklz] glasses **73 mansion** large impressive house **heap** mass of material **76 to glean** to collect or gather from various sources **76 Cliff's Notes** *Lektürehilfen für Schüler* **85/86 to be admitted to hospital** to be accepted into a hospital as a patient **86 chest** upper front part of the body **91 surgery** operation **96 to vindicate** to clear sb/sth of blame or suspicion **98 choir** [ˈkwaɪə(r)] group of people singing together **99 devastating** [ˈdevəsteɪtɪŋ] (adj) causing shock or sadness **104 impending** (adj) about to happen soon **105 sole** bottom part of the foot or shoe

Getting Behind The Lines

Arnie charted trigonometric patterns. X-axis: the function of pressure is on the rise. Y-axis: the probability exists that Arnie will be forced to use his crib notes. Z-axis: the arc of trouble in Arnie's life increases at an extremely sharp angle, the black line speeding unheeded toward infinity.

Understanding the text

Organise the answers to the following 3 questions in table form:

subject	test material	crib notes	events

1. In what subjects and on what specific material is Arnie being tested?
2. What kind of crib notes does he prepare for each test in order to help him?
3. Name all the events that prevent Arnie from studying properly for each exam.

Analysing the text

1. In what way is the test material related to Arnie's everyday problems?
2. Discuss what could be meant by "the black line speeding unheeded toward infinity."

Creative writing

Imagine what might happen on Arnie's test day and write either a comic, surprising, happy or tragic ending to the story.

---

109 to chart *zeichnerisch darstellen* **trigonometric** [trigənə'metrɪk] **111 probability** chance that a certain event will occur **112 crib notes** *Spickzettel* **arc** curve **114 angle** corner where two lines meet **to speed** to move or go quickly **unheeded** (adv) heard or noticed but not responded to **115 infinity** [ɪn'fɪnəti] state of having no end or limit

16 Literature

Pre-reading activity

Write out the following poem on a separate piece of paper. As you then read it, record your immediate responses to any words, images, phrases or lines which you wish to respond to.

Coat

Sometimes I have wanted
to throw you off
like a heavy coat.

Sometimes I have said
5 you would not let me
breathe or move.

But now that I am free
to choose light clothes
or none at all

10 I feel the cold
and all the time I think
how warm it used to be.

Vicki Feaver

Discussing the poem

1. Who or what might be represented by "you" in the 2nd and 5th lines?
2. Explain the extended metaphor based on your interpretation of "you."
3. What message do you see in this poem?

Creative writing

Write a new version of this poem using your own simile to replace "like a heavy coat." Stay in the word field of your chosen metaphor.

A **simile** ['sɪməli] is a comparison using the words "as" or "like" to link things that are often thought of as being unlike, for example "her eyes are as blue as the sea."

While a simile says that something is **like** something else, a **metaphor** ['metəfə(r)] says that something *is* something else. This can be a simple metaphor consisting of only one line ("The road is a snake") or it can be an **extended metaphor** in which qualities, characteristics and actions are transferred from one to the other ("The road is a snake, curving around the hills and rearing its head at the top of the rise, before swallowing the green fields in one gulp").

Getting Behind The Lines

Pre-reading activity Complete the following collection of words with the thematic vocabulary referring to death. Consult your dictionary.

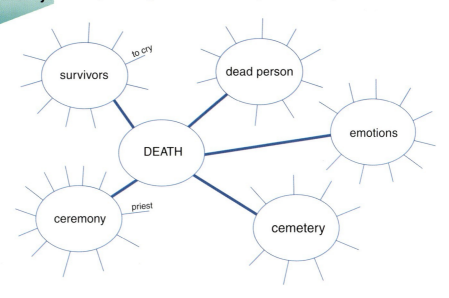

Twelve Songs

IX

Stop all the clocks, cut off the telephone,
Prevent the dog from barking with a juicy bone,
Silence the pianos and with muffled drum
Bring out the coffin, let the mourners come.

5 Let aeroplanes circle moaning overhead
Scribbling on the sky the message He Is Dead,
Put crêpe bows round the white necks of the public doves,
Let the traffic policemen wear black cotton gloves.

He was my North, my South, my East and West,
10 My working week and my Sunday rest,
My noon, my midnight, my talk, my song;
I thought that love would last for ever: I was wrong.

The stars are not wanted now; put out every one;
Pack up the moon and dismantle the sun;
15 Pour away the ocean and sweep up the wood;
For nothing now can ever come to any good.

Wystan Hugh Auden

---

3 muffled (adj) not heard clearly **4 coffin** box in which dead bodies are buried **4 mourner** ['mɔːnə] sb who is sad because someone has died **5 to moan** to make a sound as if in pain **7 bow** [bəʊ] *Schleife* **dove** [dʌv] *Taube* **15 to pour** [pɔː(r)] to let flow **to sweep up** to remove sth with a brush

 Literature

Understanding the poem
1. Sum up in *one* sentence what this poem is about.
2. How is the 3rd stanza different from the other three?
3. Which orders given by the poetic "I" can be easily followed and which ones cannot? Explain the progression here.

Discussing the poem
1. What emotions cause the poetic "I" to react the way he does?
2. Imagine what the relationship between the mourner and the dead person was like. Base your answers on the text.

Going beyond the poem
Discuss the opinions expressed in lines 12 and 16.

Pre-reading activity
Judging from this title, what do you think the short story is about?

Discovery Of A Father
Sherwood Anderson

One of the strangest relationships in the world is that between father and son. I know it now from having sons of my own.

A boy wants something very special from his 5 father. You hear it said that fathers want their sons to be what they feel they cannot themselves be, but I tell you it also works the other way. I know that as a small boy I wanted my father to be a certain thing he was not. I want- 10 ed him to be a proud, silent, dignified father. When I was with the other boys and he passed along the street, I wanted to feel a glow of pride: "There he is. That is my father."

But he wasn't such a one. He couldn't be. It seemed to me then that he was always showing 15 off. Let's say someone in our town had got up a show. They were always doing it. The druggist would be in it, the shoe-store clerk, the horse doctor, and a lot of women and girls. My father would manage to get the chief comedy 20

---

10 dignified respected, serious and important **12 glow** here: feeling of warmth **15/16 to show off** to behave proudly in order to impress others **17/18 druggist** (Brit chemist) **18 clerk** [klɑːk; US klɜːrk] person who works in an office or shop

part. It was, let's say, a Civil War play and he was a comic Irish soldier. He had to do the most absurd things. They thought he was funny, but I didn't.

I thought he was terrible. I didn't see how Mother could stand it. She even laughed with the others. Maybe I would have laughed if it hadn't been my father.

Or there was a parade, the Fourth of July or Decoration Day. He'd be in that, too, right at the front of it, as Grand Marshal or something, on a white horse hired from a livery stable.

He couldn't ride for shucks. He fell off the horse and everyone hooted with laughter, but he didn't care. He even seemed to like it. I remember once when he had done something ridiculous, and right out on Main Street, too. I was with some other boys and they were laughing and shouting at him and he was shouting back and having as good a time as they were. I ran down an alley back of some stores and there in the Presbyterian Church sheds I had a good long cry.

Or I would be in bed at night and Father would come home and bring some men with him. He was a man who was never alone. Before he went broke, running a harness shop, there were always a lot of men loafing in the shop. He went broke, of course, because he gave too much credit. He couldn't refuse it and I thought he was a fool. I had got to hating him.

There'd be men I didn't think would want to be fooling around with him. There might even be the superintendent of our schools and a quiet man who ran the hardware store. Once I remember there was a white-haired man who was a cashier of the bank. It was a wonder to me they'd want to be seen with such a windbag.

That's what I thought he was. I know now what it was that attracted them. It was because life in our town, as in all small towns was at times pretty dull and he livened it up. He made them laugh. He could tell stories. He'd even got them to singing.

If they didn't come to our house they'd go off, say at night, to where there was a grassy place by a creek. They'd cook food there and drink beer and sit about listening to his stories.

He was always telling stories about himself.

---

30 Decoration Day (usu Memorial Day) the last Monday in May: day for remembering soldiers killed in battle **31 Grand Marshal** person in charge of a public event like a parade **32 livery stable** [ˈlɪvəri] place where horses are kept for owners or where horses can be hired **33 cannot do sth for shucks** (infml) cannot do sth very well **34 to hoot** to shout or cry out **37 ridiculous** [rɪˈdɪkjələs] stupid, foolish, silly **41 alley** [ˈæli] long, narrow passage, usu between or behind houses **42 Presbyterian Church** [ˌprezbɪˈtɪəriən] branch of the Protestant church **47 harness** *Pferdegeschirr* **48 to loaf** to stand about doing nothing **49 to go broke** (infml) to run out of money **51 I had got to hating him** (non-standard) I had begun to hate him **54 superintendent** [ˌ---ˈ--] person who controls the schools in one district **55 hardware store** shop that sells metal tools and household goods (eg hammers, locks, nails) **57 cashier** person who handles money in a shop or bank **58 windbag** (derog, infml) person who talks too much **62 dull** here: boring **to liven sb/sth up** [ˈlaɪvn] to cause sb/sth to have/be more fun **67 creek** small stream of water

He'd say this or that wonderful thing had happened to him. It might be something that made him look like a fool. He didn't care.

If an Irishman came to our house, right away Father would say he was Irish. He'd tell what county in Ireland he was born in. He'd tell things that happened there when he was a boy. He'd make it seem so real that, if I hadn't known he was born in southern Ohio, I'd have believed him myself.

If it was a Scotchman the same thing happened. He'd get a burr into his speech. Or he was a German or a Swede. He'd be anything the other man was. I think they all knew he was lying, but they seemed to like him just the same. As a boy that was what I couldn't understand. And there was Mother. How could she stand it? I wanted to ask but never did. She was not the kind you asked such questions.

I'd be upstairs in my bed, in my room above the porch and Father would be telling some of his tales. A lot of Father's stories were about the Civil War. To hear him tell it he'd been in about every battle. He'd known Grant, Sherman, Sheridan and I don't know how many others. He'd been particularly intimate with General Grant, so that when Grant went East, to take charge of all the armies, he took Father along. "I was an orderly at headquarters and Sam Grant said to me, 'Irve,' he said, 'I'm going to take you along with me.'"

It seems he and Grant used to slip off sometimes and have a quiet drink together. That's what my father said. He'd tell about the day Lee surrendered and how, when the great moment came, they couldn't find Grant.

"You know," my father said, "about General Grant's book, his memoirs. You've read of how he said he had a headache and how, when he got word that Lee was ready to call it quits, he was suddenly and miraculously cured."

"Huh," said Father. "He was in the woods with me."

"I was in there with my back against a tree. I was drinking. I had got hold of a bottle."

"They were looking for Grant. He had got off his horse and come into the woods. He found me. He was covered with mud."

"I had the bottle in my hand. What'd I care? The war was over. I knew we had them licked."

My father said that he was the one who told Grant about Lee. An orderly riding by had told him, because the orderly knew how thick he was with Grant. Grant was embarrassed.

"But, Irve, look at me. I'm covered with mud," he said to Father.

And then, my father said, he and Grant decided to have a drink together. They took a couple of drinks and then, because he didn't want Grant to show up drunk before the immaculate Lee, he smashed the bottle against the tree.

"Sam Grant's dead now and I wouldn't want it to get out on him," my father said.

That's just one of the kind of things he'd tell. Of course the men knew he was lying, but they seemed to like it just the same.

When we got broke, down and out, do you think he ever brought anything home? Not he. If there wasn't anything to eat in the house, he'd go off visiting around at farmhouses. They all wanted him. Sometimes he'd stay away for weeks. Mother working to keep us fed, and then home he'd come bringing, let's say, a ham. He'd got it from some farmer friend. He'd slap it on the table in the kitchen. "You bet I'm going to see that my kids have something to eat," he'd say, and Mother would just stand smiling at him. She'd never say a word about

---

81 burr here: accent with a strong pronunciation of the "r" sound **90 porch** (US) veranda **93 Ulysses S. Grant** (1822–85), William Tecumseh **Sherman** (1820–91), Phillip Henry **Sheridan** (1831–88) Union generals in the Civil War; Grant became the 18th President of the US **96/97 to take charge of sb/sth** to become responsible for sb/sth **98 orderly** here: soldier who does small duties for an officer **101 to slip off** (infml) to go away quietly and secretly **104** Robert E. **Lee** (1807–70) Confederate general in the Civil War **to surrender** to stop fighting and accept that one's enemy has won **107 memoirs** ['memwɑːs] written description of one's life **110 miraculous** [-'---] surprising and sudden **cured** brought back to good health **119 to lick** here: (sl) to beat **122 to be thick with sb** (infml) to be very good friends with sb **123 embarrassed** feeling awkward or ashamed **129 immaculate** [ɪ'mækjʊlət] very clean and neat **132 to get out on sb** to make information about sb known publicly **136 to get broke** (non-standard) to go broke; to lose all one's money **143 to slap sth down** to put sth down with a lot of force or carelessly

all the weeks and months he'd been away, not leaving us a cent for food. Once I heard her speaking to a woman in our street. Maybe the woman had dared to sympathize with her. "Oh," she said, "it's all right. He isn't ever dull like most of the men in this street. Life is never dull when my man is about."

But often I was filled with bitterness, and sometimes I wished he wasn't my father. I'd even invent another man as my father. To protect my mother I'd make up stories of a secret marriage that for some strange reason never got known. As though some man, say the president of a railroad company or maybe a Congressman, he married my mother, thinking his wife was dead and then it turned out she wasn't.

So they had to hush it up but I got born just the same. I wasn't really the son of my father. Somewhere in the world there was a very dignified, quite wonderful man who was really my father. I even made myself half believe these fancies.

And then there came a certain night. Mother was away from home. Maybe there was church that night. Father came in. He'd been off somewhere for two or three weeks. He found me alone in the house, reading by the kitchen table.

It had been raining and he was very wet. He sat and looked at me for a long time, not saying a word. I was startled, for there was on his face the saddest look I had ever seen. He sat for a time, his clothes dripping. Then he got up.

"Come on with me," he said.

I got up and went with him out of the house. I was filled with wonder but I wasn't afraid.

We went along a dirt road that led down into a valley, about a mile out of town, where there was a pond. We walked in silence. The man who was always talking had stopped his talking.

I didn't know what was up and had the queer feeling that I was with a stranger. I don't know whether my father intended it so. I don't think he did.

The pond was quite large. It was still raining hard and there were flashes of lightning followed by thunder. We were on a grassy bank at the pond's edge when my father spoke, and in the darkness and rain his voice sounded strange.

"Take off your clothes," he said. Still filled with wonder, I began to undress. There was a flash of lightning and I saw that he was already naked.

Naked, we went into the pond. Taking my hand he pulled me in. It may be that I was too frightened, too full of a feeling of strangeness, to speak. Before that night my father had never seemed to pay any attention to me. "And what is he up to now?" I kept asking myself. I did not swim very well, but he put my hand on his shoulder and struck out into the darkness.

He was a man with big shoulders, a powerful swimmer. In the darkness I could feel the movement of his muscles. We swam to the far edge of the pond and then back to where we had left our clothes. The rain continued and the wind blew. Sometimes my father swam on his back and when he did he took my hand in his large powerful one and moved it over so that it rested always on his shoulder. Sometimes there would be a flash of lightning and I could see his face quite clearly.

It was as it was earlier, in the kitchen, a face filled with sadness. There would be the

---

164 to hush sth up to stop sth from becoming known publicly **169 fancy** imagined event or thing **178 to startle** to surprise **186 pond** small lake **189 queer** here: strange, odd, peculiar **195 bank** here: land on either side of a river or lake **202 naked** ['neɪkɪd]

momentary glimpse of his face and then again the darkness, the wind and the rain. In me there was a feeling I had never known before.

It was a feeling of closeness. It was something strange. It was as though there were only we two in the world. It was as though I had been jerked suddenly out of myself, out of my world of the schoolboy, out of a world in which I was ashamed of my father.

He had become blood of my blood; he the strong swimmer and I the boy clinging to him in the darkness. We swam in silence and in silence we dressed in our wet clothes, and went home.

There was a lamp lighted in the kitchen and when we came in, the water dripping from us, there was my mother. She smiled at us. I remember that she called us "boys." "What have you boys been up to?" she asked, but my father did not answer. As he had begun the evening's experience with me in silence, so he ended it. He turned and looked at me. Then he went, I thought, with a new and a strange dignity, out of the room.

I climbed the stairs to my own room, undressed in darkness and got into bed. I couldn't sleep and did not want to sleep. For the first time I knew that I was the son of my father. He was a storyteller as I was to be. It may be that I even laughed a little softly there in the darkness. If I did, I laughed knowing that I would never again be wanting another father.

Understanding the text

1. Point out the different episodes in the story. Summarise each one briefly.
2. What do we know about the narrator?
3. Describe the boy's attitude towards his father and how it changes.

---

224 glimpse [glɪmps] quick, short look **230 to jerk** to pull quickly (here: fig use) **234 to cling** (pt, pp clung) to hold tightly **246/247 dignity** state of being formal, serious and important; *Würde*

Internet Sherwood Anderson → http://www.nwohio.com/clydeoh/sherwood.htm

Getting Behind The Lines

Analysing the text

1. What point of view is used?
2. Who is the protagonist in this story: the father or the son? Give reasons for your opinion.
3. Explain the symbolic meaning of the pond and the storm in the final episode.

> The **protagonist** in a story is the central or main character. At the end of the story, it is the protagonist who has been changed by the central conflict.

Pre-reading activity

What would you not like to lose?

One Art

The art of losing isn't hard to master;
so many things seem filled with the intent
to be lost that their loss is no disaster.

Lose something every day. Accept the fluster
5 of lost door keys, the hour badly spent.
The art of losing isn't hard to master.

Then practice losing farther, losing faster:
places, and names, and where it was you meant
to travel. None of these will bring disaster.

10 I lost my mother's watch. And look! my last, or
next-to-last, of three loved houses went.
The art of losing isn't hard to master.

I lost two cities, lovely ones. And, vaster,
some realms I owned, two rivers, a continent.
15 I miss them, but it wasn't a disaster.

– Even losing you (the joking voice, a gesture
I love) I shan't have lied. It's evident
the art of losing's not too hard to master
though it may look like (*Write* it!) like disaster.

Elizabeth Bishop

---

2 intent [-'-] intention, purpose **4 fluster** state of being nervous and confused **8 to mean to do sth** to plan to do sth **13 vast** very large in area, size, degree **14 realm** [relm] (fml or rhet) a country ruled by a king or a queen **17 evident** ['---] clear

Literature

Understanding the poem

1. What kind of losses does the poetic "I" mention? List them.
2. Which recurring words seem to be keywords for understanding the message of this poem? Formulate this message in your own words.

Analysing the poem

1. Comment on the structure of this poem, i.e. on its form, stanzas, rhyme scheme and sentence structure.
2. When read aloud, the sound quality of this villanelle has quite a hypnotic effect on the audience. What is responsible for this?
3. How does the tone of the poem change in the last stanza? Why?

Discussing the poem

1. Discuss why the poetic "I" does not regard most losses as a disaster.
2. Why does the poetic "I" call the act of losing something an "art"?

Going beyond the poem

What do the poems "One Art" and "Twelve Songs (IX)" have in common?

Working with the language

Work in groups. Collect as many idioms and phrasal verbs as possible using the verb "to lose."

Rhyme occurs when two words have the same sound in their stressed syllable, e.g. "funny" rhymes with "honey," "head" with "led." In a poem, rhyme usually occurs at the end of lines (known as **end rhyme** or **external rhyme**) and occasionally a poet may use it within a line (known as **internal rhyme**).

A **rhyme scheme** is the pattern of rhymes in a poem (the first rhyme is given the letter 'a,' the second 'b' etc).

A **villanelle** [vɪləˈnɛl] consists of 6 stanzas; the first 5 stanzas are three lines long and the final stanza is four lines long. The first line and last line of the first stanza take turns repeating as the final line of the next four stanzas, and then are rejoined as the last two lines of the poem. The poem has a rhyme scheme of a, b, a throughout, except in the last stanza where there is a slight variation.

The **tone** reflects the author's emotional attitude towards the subject, theme, characters, situation and reader. A writer's tone (e.g. formal, intimate, serious, playful, ironic, sarcastic, humorous, angry, critical, arrogant etc) may change within a text depending upon the theme, character or situation being dealt with at that moment.

Getting Behind The Lines

Pre-reading activity Describe the situation depicted in the cartoon.

The Tiny Closet
William Inge

SCENE: *A boarding-rooming house somewhere in a Midwestern city. On stage we see the big living room of the house, which is Victorian in design, with ornate woodwork and high ceiling. The furnishings, too, are Victorian. An ornate wooden stairway is at the Right. The outside entrance is Down Right. When the curtain is up, MR. NEWBOLD is seen coming down the stairs. He is a man of about fifty, a large man and rather nice looking. He is always impeccably dressed in the most conservative clothes, a dark blue suit, white shirt, modest tie, a high shine on his black shoes, and his thinning hair carefully combed. He is the sort of man who takes great pride in his grooming. Something now seems to be bothering him. When he gets to the bottom of the stairs, he stops a moment and thinks. Then he calls his landlady.*

MR. NEWBOLD. Mrs. Crosby! *(No response.)* Mrs. Crosby!

MRS. CROSBY *(coming from the kitchen).* Yes,

---

tiny very small **closet** ['klɒzɪt] (esp US) small room for storing things **1 scene** [siːn] here: place represented on the theatre stage **3 Victorian** dating from Queen Victoria's time (1837–1901) **4 ornate** [ɔːˈneɪt] very fancy, richly decorated **11 impeccable** [ɪmˈpekəbl] free from mistakes **16 grooming** *gepflegtes Äußeres* **17 to bother** [ˈbɒðə] to worry sb

Mr. Newbold. I was just straightening up after breakfast. I'm afraid none of the guests like the new bacon I got. It's just as expensive as the other bacon I was serving. On my word it is. Every bit. I didn't buy it to bring down expenses. Not at all. It's fine bacon. Hickory smoked. Only it's the kind you slice yourself. That's why I got it. You can cut yourself a good thick slice of bacon that you can really get your teeth into, instead of that other stuff that shrivels up like tissue paper ... *(She is the sort of woman who continues talking until someone stops her.)*

MR. NEWBOLD Mrs. Crosby ...

MRS. CROSBY. Yes, Mr. Newbold?

MR. NEWBOLD. Mrs. Crosby, you remember, before I moved in, I specified that no one was to enter my closet ...

MRS. CROSBY. Indeed I remember, Mr. Newbold. And I told you, you could have your own lock on the closet, like you asked me. No one around here has any keys to your closet but you, Mr. Newbold.

MR. NEWBOLD. Nevertheless, Mrs. Crosby ...

MRS. CROSBY. And I told the cleaning woman, "Elsie, you're not to enter Mr. Newbold's closet. Mr. Newbold," I told her, "is a perfectly orderly gentleman who is perfectly capable of keeping his own closet, and you're not to bother it." I gave her strict orders, Mr. Newbold.

MR. NEWBOLD. Nevertheless. Mrs. Crosby ...

MRS. CROSBY. And as for me, goodness, I never go near the rooms. I got enough on my hands downstairs without bothering about the upstairs. I leave all that to Elsie. I don't suppose I been upstairs now in almost ...

MR. NEWBOLD. Mrs. Crosby, a closet is a very small space. That's all I ask in this life. That's all I ask, is just that tiny closet to call my own, my very own.

MRS. CROSBY. I quite understand, Mr. Newbold. We all have to have some place that's private to us, where we don't invite the world to see. I quite understand.

MR. NEWBOLD. But someone has been monkeying with the lock on the door. Mrs. Crosby.

MRS. CROSBY. *(shocked).* You don't say!

MR. NEWBOLD. I *do* say, Mrs. Crosby. Someone has been monkeying with that expensive Yale lock I had put on the door.

MRS. CROSBY. Do you suppose someone coulda got up there when no one was around and ...

MR. NEWBOLD. I'm sure I don't know, but I won't stand for anyone's monkeying with that lock, Mrs. Crosby. That room, while I rent it, is my private property, and I gave strict instructions that no one was to go near the closet, and I expect my orders to be respected.

MRS. CROSBY. Of course, Mr. Newbold; you're my favorite of all the roomers. Oh, I wish they was all like you. You keep your room spotless, and you're always so correct around the house. My, you're a model guest. You really are. You should open up a class out here at that night school they have for adults and teach 'em how to behave in their rooming houses. The landladies in this town would get together and thank you.

MR. NEWBOLD. Thank you, Mrs. Crosby. Nevertheless, I must repeat that that closet is my personal property. There is nothing inside I am ashamed of. It's not that. It's only that I have some place, just some little place, that's completely private, that no one has access to. That's all I ask, Mrs. Crosby.

MRS. CROSBY. And I quite understand, Mr. Newbold.

MR. NEWBOLD. Very well. As long as that is clearly understood, I hope I'll not have to bring the subject up again, Mrs. Crosby.

MRS. CROSBY. I'll tell Elsie again, Mr. Newbold. I'll give special emphasis that no one is to go near that closet.

---

29 hickory smoked prepared by smoking with hickory wood (hickory: a North American tree) **33 to shrivel** [ˈʃrɪvl] *schrumpfen* **tissue paper** [ˈtɪʃuː] very thin soft paper used for wrapping things **72 to monkey with sth** (infml) to play or interfere with sth (in a careless manner) **73 Yale lock** type of lock; "Yale" is the brand name **75 coulda got** (non-standard) could have got

Getting Behind The Lines

Mr. Newbold. Thank you, Mrs. Crosby. *(Looks at his watch.)* Goodness! I mustn't dally another minute.

Mrs. Crosby. Did you see Mrs. Hergesheimer in your store yesterday, Mr. Newbold?

Mr. Newbold. Mrs. Hergesheimer? Oh, yes, I believe I did.

Mrs. Crosby. She called me yesterday and told me she seen you. "Whata fine man that Mr. Newbold is!" she says. "You're a lucky woman, Mrs. Crosby, to have such a fine guest. All I got in my house is a lotta old-maid schoolteachers, and I'm always cleaning up after them." That's what she says. "Oh, men are much tidier than women," I told her. I kept schoolteachers once, and they was always in the bathroom, curling their hair in there or giving themselves shampoos, or shaving their legs on my nice bedspreads. Mr. Crosby was alive then, and it almost drove him crazy. He never could get to the bathroom when he wanted to, because of them schoolteachers.

Mr. Newbold. Good day, Mrs. Crosby. *(He puts on his hat and goes out the door.)*

Mrs. Crosby. Good day, Mr. Newbold! *(Calling to him outside the door.)* You be here for dinner tonight, won't you?

Mr. Newbold. *(off).* I intend to be.

Mrs. Crosby. *(closing the door.)* Good day, Mr. Newbold.

[Now she comes back inside the room. Curiosity is about to kill her. She is childishly excited. She goes back to the door and peers out to make sure that Mr. Newbold is on his way. Then she comes back inside the room and goes to the telephone, dialing her number.]

Mrs. Crosby. Mrs. Hergesheimer? Have you got a minute? He's just left. "You're not to go into my room," he says to me again, for the two-hundredth time. "Someone's been playing with the lock on my door, and you're not to go near that closet," he says, like it was his house and he was ordering me about. Can you beat it? Now what do you suppose he's got hid away in that closet? *(She listens a while.)* No, I can't think he'd be a Communist, Mrs. Hergesheimer. Of course, he might be. You never can tell. But I don't think that's it, somehow. *(She listens again.)* Love letters? But why would he need a whole closet for his love letters? – If he's got any. Besides, I don't think he's the type of man that has love letters. *(She listens.)* It's certainly a mystery. I confess, it's certainly a mystery. What would you do, Mrs. Hergesheimer? *(A pause.)* You would? Well, hurry over, why don't you, and we'll try again. Hurry! *(She hangs up, then calls out to the kitchen.)* Elsie, you're not to go upstairs for a while. Mrs. Hergesheimer is comin' over, and she and I have some things we wanta do up there, so you're to keep busy with the washin'. Understand?

Elsie *(off)* Yes, Mrs. Crosby.

[Now Mrs. Crosby spends a few minutes of nervous activity. Her conscience bothers her some, but primarily she is afraid of being caught. She looks out the door again, then out of each window; then calls out to the kitchen again.]

Mrs. Crosby. Remember, Elsie, you're not to bother me for a while. I'll let you know when I want you, Elsie. You're to stay out there till I call you.

[Now Mrs. Hergesheimer hurries into the house.]

Mrs. Hergesheimer. I think you've got every right, Mrs. Crosby. Every right.

Mrs. Crosby. That's what I've been telling myself, Mrs. Hergesheimer. I've got every right. For all I know, I may be harboring a spy, or a criminal, or a lunatic. What's he got in that closet that he don't want anyone to see? Can you tell me? It must be something

---

111 to dally to waste time **117 whata** (non-standard) what a **120 lotta** (non-standard) lot of **172 wanta** (non-standard) want to **176 conscience** [ˈkɒnʃəns] awareness of what is good or bad, right or wrong **191 to harbor** (Brit harbour) to give shelter to, to protect **192 lunatic** [ˈluːnətɪk] mad person

he's ashamed of, or he wouldn't mind if anyone saw. Isn't that what you say? And if it's something he's ashamed of, I think we should find out what it is. You can't tell – he might have a bomb in there he meant to destroy us with. I'm not gonna set idly by while someone is plotting something, Mrs. Hergesheimer. I pride myself I'm a real American, and I say if anyone's got any secrets he wants to keep hid, let 'm come out into the open and declare himself. Mr. Newbold has always seemed like a fine man, and I got nothin' against him personally, and he's the best roomer I ever had; keeps his room spotless. Elsie don't have to do anything but make the bed. And I appreciate that, but if you ask me, it's kinda unnatural for a man to be so tidy. Isn't that what you say? There's been something suspicious about him from the very first.

MRS. HERGESHEIMER. I made a point of talking to him when I was shopping in Baumgarden's yesterday. My, he struts around that floor. You'd think he was president instead of a floorwalker. I asked him where they kept the artificial flowers. I knew, but I just wanted to see if he'd recognize me. He smiled and made a lordly gesture with his hand, showin' me the way. You'd have thought he was the king of Persia, with all his fine manners.

MRS. CROSBY. He belongs to the Lions Club. Do you think he'd be a Communist and still belong to the Lions Club?

MRS. HERGESHEIMER. You can't tell. Lots of them join clubs like that just as a cover-up. That schoolteacher I got – she's a Red and I know it. Brings home all kinds of books to read. Yes. Dangerous books. But she goes to church every Sunday morning, just as big as you please, just to pretend she's *not* a Red.

MRS. CROSBY. Forevermore!

MRS. HERGESHEIMER. I think you've got every right to go into that closet, Mrs. Crosby.

MRS. CROSBY. Yes, I think so, too. Well – well, you come with me!

MRS. HERGESHEIMER. Oh. Mrs. Crosby, honey, I don't think it's right for me to do it. I'll stay down here and see that Elsie doesn't bother you.

MRS. CROSBY. I'm not going to do it if you don't come with me.

MRS. HERGESHEIMER. Well ...

MRS. CROSBY. After all you've been just as curious about this as I've been, and I think you owe it to me to come along.

MRS. HERGESHEIMER. Well, if that's the way you feel about it, Mrs. Crosby, I'll come along. After all, it's not as though we were doing anything criminal.

MRS. CROSBY. Indeed it's not. Come on, then.
[She starts toward the stairs, taking a final look toward the kitchen to make sure that Elsie is occupied.]

MRS. HERGESHEIMER *(following with some trepidation)*. O dear, I hope he doesn't find out.

MRS. CROSBY. We can get that lock off this time without making any more scratches than we made yesterday. He won't notice.

MRS. HERGESHEIMER. Oh, I bet he does. He's got a sharp eye.

MRS. CROSBY. Well, I don't care if he does. I've got a right to see what's in that closet.

MRS. HERGESHEIMER. Yes. Well – go on, Mrs. Crosby. I'm right behind you.
[Slowly, cautiously, the two women go up the stairs together. The stage is empty for a few

---

200 gonna set by (non-standard) going to sit by (to take no action to stop sth bad happening) **idle** ['aɪdl] not active **201 to plot** to plan in secret **204 let 'm** (contraction) let him **210 to appreciate** here: to understand or realise sth **213 suspicious** [sə'spɪʃəs] here: odd or strange **217 to strut** to walk in an upright, proud way **219 floorwalker** (US) person employed in a store to help customers **226 Lions Club** society founded in 1917 in Dallas to help poor people and organise social and community programmes **231 Red** (infml) a Communist **244 to bother sb** here: to trouble or annoy sb **251 to owe sth to sb** [əʊ] *jdm etwas schulden* **260/261 trepidation** [trepɪ'deɪʃn] great worry or fear **263 scratch** small cut

moments, then Elsie comes in from the kitchen, looks up the stairs with curiosity. Then, as though the behavior of the two women were too much for her to understand, she shrugs her shoulders, laughs gently, and returns to the kitchen. The stage is empty again for a few moments. Then, slowly, the front door opens and Mr. Newbold returns inside the house. He has suspected the two women would do exactly what they're doing. He is very nervous. His heart is pounding. He starts up the stairs and then comes down again. He can't seem to get the courage to confront the women. The starch he showed earlier in the play has dissolved. He is perspiring heavily and twisting his hands in fear and excitement. In a few moments we hear the women on their way downstairs. Mr. Newbold hurriedly finds a closet to hide him. The women come down the stairs slowly, holding an awed silence. Mrs. Crosby carries a woman's hat, a large hat, the kind a graceful lady might wear to a garden party. It is quite a lovely hat, in a light pastel color with great flowers in its limber brim, and sleek satin ribbons. They come together, Mrs. Crosby holding the hat, both of them studying it with bafflement.]

MRS. CROSBY. Hats! Dozens of hats! I can't believe it.

MRS. HERGESHEIMER. He must have brought them home from the store, don't you think?

MRS. CROSBY. But there was all that sewing equipment on a shelf.

MRS. HERGESHEIMER. But no man could make hats as lovely as these.

MRS. CROSBY. I don't know. There's something kinda unusual about Mr. Newbold. I think he might have made them. I – I know he did. *(She suddenly recalls a clue.)* I remember now how he was always looking through the fashion magazines. Sometimes he'd take them up to his room. He'd *study* them. I always wondered why.

MRS. HERGESHEIMER. But why would he stay up in his room making hats – and then keep them locked in his closet?

MRS. CROSBY. He – he's just peculiar. That's all. He's just peculiar. I thought so, the first time I saw the man. He's too prim for a man. He's too tidy, the way he keeps his room. It's just not natural.

MRS. HERGESHEIMER. Oh, I wish now we hadn't looked.

MRS. CROSBY. I had a perfect right.

MRS. HERGESHEIMER. I know, but ...

MRS. CROSBY. Why, I think he's the most peculiar man I ever heard of. Why, I'd rather be harboring a Communist.

MRS. HERGESHEIMER. Oh, Mrs. Crosby, don't say that.

MRS. CROSBY. I would. I'd rather be harboring a Communist than a man who makes hats.

MRS. HERGESHEIMER. Why, there's nothing wrong with making hats. I don't see anything wrong with it. Why, lots of men make hats. Some of the finest designers there are are men. Why, of course.

MRS. CROSBY. But he kept them locked in his closet. He was ashamed of them.

MRS. HERGESHEIMER. Maybe it's just a hobby with him. Some men knit, you know, because it helps their nerves.

MRS. CROSBY. I'm going to ask him to leave.

MRS. HERGESHEIMER. Oh no, Mrs. Crosby. Don't do that.

MRS. CROSBY. I am. I'm going to ask him to leave. And I'm going to call the store he

---

286 starch here: *steifes Auftreten* **287 to dissolve** [dɪˈzɒlv] to disappear **287/288 to perspire** [pəˈspaɪə(r)] (fml) to sweat **288 to twist** to turn round and round **293 awed** [ɔːd] (adj) filled with wonder or fear **297 limber** flexible **298 sleek** smooth and shiny **ribbon** *Band* **300 bafflement** state of not understanding or being puzzled **305 sewing** [ˈsəʊɪŋ] the making of clothes etc with needle and thread **310 kinda** (non-standard) kind of **312 clue** fact that helps to solve a problem; *Hinweis* **322 prim** (usu derog) stiffly formal; disliking anything that is improper, rude or rough **344 to knit** *stricken*

works at and tell them what kind of a freak they have working for them. Indeed I am.
MRS. HERGESHEIMER. Oh, I wouldn't do that. It's not against the law for a man to make hats. He hasn't done anything really wrong.
MRS. CROSBY. Why, a man who'd make hats and lock them up in his closet, there's no telling what kind of a person he is. He might do any kind of dangerous, crazy thing.
MRS. HERGESHEIMER. Oh, I don't think so, Mrs. Crosby. Really I don't.
MRS. CROSBY. I'd rather he was a Communist. At least you know what a Communist is up to. But a man that makes hats! What can you tell about such a creature?
MRS. HERGESHEIMER. I wouldn't give it another thought, if I was you.
MRS. CROSBY. Well, I guess it takes all kinds of people to make a world.
MRS. HERGESHEIMER. Of course. That's the way to look at it.
MRS. CROSBY. Hats! Hats! Hats! With flowers on them.
MRS. HERGESHEIMER. I must run along now.
MRS. CROSBY. Hats!
MRS. HERGESHEIMER. Goodness, I hope he never finds out ...
MRS. CROSBY. I don't care if he does. Just let him try to scold me in that superior way of his *(Imitating Mr. Newbold.)* "Mrs. Crosby, someone's been tampering with the lock on my closet. I demand privacy, Mrs. Crosby. That's all I ask is just one tiny closet to call my own. That's all I ask." Hmm. I'll have an answer for him. "What in God's name does a grown-up man like you mean by making hats, Mr. Newbold? Shame!" That's what I'll tell him. And he won't act so superior then.
[Mrs. Hergesheimer flutters out of the house as though wanting to avoid further involvement. Mrs. Crosby studies the hat again, taking it to the mirror to try it on. She deliberately burlesques its elegance and all that it signifies of feminine daintiness and beauty. Then, she tosses it onto a chair and returns to the kitchen. Stealthily, Mr. Newbold comes from the closet in which he has been hiding. He is a shattered man. His stiff pride, his erect authority, are destroyed. He picks up the hat lovingly, holding it in the air to admire again its loveliness. He even weeps. Finally, his courage restored, he determines on a course of action. Twisting a great beaded hat-pin from the feathers and furbelows of his creation, he walks boldly to the kitchen door and stands, holding the pin behind his back, and calling in a voice that is eerie with its dire purpose.]
MR. NEWBOLD. Mrs. Crosby! Could you come here a moment, please? Could you come here a moment, Mrs. Crosby?

Understanding the text

1. What information is given in the stage directions?
2. How many parts can the play be divided into? Summarise each section in one complete sentence.
3. What kind of man is Mr. Newbold? Look at the stage directions, what the two women say about him, what he says about himself and how he acts.

---

351 freak [friːk] (infml, derog) person considered unusual or not normal in behaviour and/or appearance **379 to scold** to speak critically **381 to tamper with sth** to change sth without permission **389 to flutter** to move in a quick, irregular way **393 deliberate** [dɪˈlɪbərət] (adj) on purpose, intentionally **393 to burlesque** [bɜːˈlesk] to imitate or mimic **394 daintiness** *Zartheit* **395 to toss** to throw carelessly **396 stealthily** [ˈstelθɪlɪ] in a quiet way or secretly **399 erect** [-ˈ-] upright and stiff **402 to weep** to cry **404 beaded hat-pin** [ˈbiːdɪd] long pin used to fasten a hat to the hair; usually decorated with beads (small coloured balls of glass or wood) **405 furbelow** [ˈfɜːbɪləʊ] (derog) unnecessary ornaments **408 eerie** [ˈɪərɪ] causing a feeling of mystery or fear; *unheimlich* **dire** (fml) dreadful, terrible

Getting Behind The Lines

Analysing the text
1. How is suspense created in the play?
2. Characterise the two women, listing their similarities and differences.

Discussing the text
1. How did you react to the characters' actions?
2. In what way were the characters' actions predictable?
3. To what extent were you surprised by what they did?
4. What is Mr. Newbold's intention at the end of the play?

Going beyond the text
The play has an open ending. Suggest some comic and tragic endings.

The **setting** is the place, time and social surroundings in which the action of a story or play takes place. In the theatre, the scenery (or backdrops) on the stage shows the audience the location of the play. The actors' costumes and props (stage properties) such as furniture etc communicate the social milieu to the spectators.

The **stage directions** describe what should be on stage at the beginning of a scene. They may also offer details about the characters. Stage directions are not intended for the audience, but are used by actors, directors and designers as guides for presenting the play.

The **action** of a play is the answer to the question "What happened?" Dramatic action often comes from the conflict between people or between opposing beliefs and principles. There can also be a conflict within one person as he struggles with his conscience. The **actions** of the characters are the individual movements they make on stage.

The **climax** of a play is reached when the main conflict is so intense that it has to be resolved; that is, the action has to go one way or the other. Occurring shortly before the final resolution, the climax is usually the highest point of interest for the audience or reader.

Suspense is the feeling that arises from the action of the play as the audience wonders what will happen next. This feeling may be of pleasurable excitement and anticipation or of anxiety and apprehension resulting from an uncertain, undecided, or mysterious situation. The suspense leads up to a climax before the final resolution.

Characterisation is the way a character is presented on the stage or in writing, especially by imitating or describing actions, gestures, or speeches. The writer may treat the different characters as either "round" or "flat" characters, that is, they are described in detail as "real" people or simply as stereotypes.

Literature

Pre-reading activity

Work in small groups. Collect and write down popular definitions of what love is. Choose the one you like most and give reasons for your choice.

The Rose

Some say love it is a river that drowns the tender reed.
Some say love it is a razor that leaves your soul to bleed.
Some say love it is a hunger, an endless aching need.
I say love it is a flower and you it's only seed.

5 It's the heart afraid of breaking that never learns to dance.
It's the dream afraid of waking that never takes the chance.
It's the one who won't be taken, who cannot seem to give.
And the soul afraid of dying that never learns to live.

When the night has been too lonely and the road has been too long,
10 And you think that love is only for the lucky and the strong,
Just remember in the winter far beneath the bitter snows
lies the seed that with the sun's love in the spring becomes the rose.

Amanda McBroom
Fox Fanfare Music Inc. NEUE WELT MUSIKVERLAG GMBH, München

Understanding the song

1. Find all the metaphors that convey a negative definition of love to the reader.
2. What psychological reasons for such negative attitudes are mentioned in the song?
3. How are lines 4 and 12 linked with each other?

Analysing the song

1. Describe relationships in which one partner might compare love to a river, a razor, a hunger.
2. What advice does the singer give the listener in the last two lines?

Going beyond the song

1. Write a dialogue between two friends about love using the two lines of argument put forward in this song. One person believes in love, the other does not.
2. Bring in the lyrics of your favourite song and present them to the class. Discuss the poetic qualities of the lyrics.

Lyric (singular) was identified by Greek writers as a song composed to the accompaniment of a **lyre**, an old musical instrument. Today the term **lyric** is used for any fairly short, non-narrative poem representing a single speaker who expresses his feelings. A **lyric poem** may therefore be simply a brief expression of a mood or state of feeling. **Lyrics** (plural) refer to the words of a song and a **lyricist** is a person who writes the words of songs.

1 to drown sb/sth [aʊ] to kill sb/sth by covering with water **tender** soft, easily damaged or hurt **reed** tall grass growing near water **2 razor** sharp instrument used for shaving **3 to ache** [eɪk] to suffer from a continuous pain **4 seed** part of a plant that will grow into a new one

The South: More Than Just A Region

Top: Catalpa Plantation in Louisiana. Above left: A cotton harvest in Arkansas. Above right: Southerners relive a Civil War battle campaign. Center: A jazz band plays at a club in New Orleans.

 The South

Getting to know the South

Take the first letter of the first 12 answers and you will be able to spell the answer to number 13.

1. After the Civil War was over in 1865, slavery was ? ? ?, meaning it did not exist any more.
2. Martin Luther King Jr used principles of non-violent civil disobedience which were first used by the great nationalist leader of India, Mohatma ? ? ?.
3. The goal of the Civil ? ? ? movement in the 1950s and 1960s was to put an end to racial prejudice.
4. The opposite of "segregation" is ? ? ?.
5. The eleven states which broke off from the United States in the 1860s were called the ? ? ? States of America.
6. During the Civil War the northern states were called the ? ? ?.
7. Southern planters wanted to keep the old tradition of slave ? ? ? for their plantations.
8. New ? ? ? were settled on the western frontier in the first half of the 1800s.
9. Before the Civil Rights movement, minorities were not allowed to attend white schools or ? ? ?.
10. The second longest natural waterway in America is the Mississippi ? ? ?.
11. The southern city of ? ? ? hosted the 1996 Summer Olympic games.
12. President Abraham ? ? ? was shot and killed in April, 1885.
13. When America was settled, the northern economy built up an industrial economy and the South had an ? ? ? economy.

Internet

The South →
http://www.olemiss.edu/depts/south

More Than Just A Region

A Unique History

What Is So Different About The South?
Five People, Five Different Answers

If you travel through the southeastern United States today, you will see houses and people, fields and highways, fast-food chains and skyscrapers that all look about the same as anywhere else in America. But if you ask five different Americans if there is anything that makes the South different from the rest of the country, you may get five different answers.

One person might mention how the South was settled mostly by British immigrants who wanted to get as much as they could from the land. After they found no gold, they became farmers, noticing how the warm climate was well-suited for growing crops such as tobacco, sugar-cane, rice and cotton. Up in New England, he'll tell you, the colonists became more specialized in trade and industry. So that's the difference: Southerners are attached to the land.

Another person might say slavery made the difference. Brought over to work on the ever-expanding plantations, the African-Americans never really became integrated into society. And ever since slavery was abolished, they'll say, the southern whites have had a hard time accepting them as equals. That's what the Civil Rights struggle was about, they'll tell you.

Yet another person will tell you the difference between a real Southerner and any other American is that he – or at least his forefathers – lost a war which was fought on his own territory. Yes, she'll say, the Civil War – which has never been forgotten in the South – made the difference: Southerners always talk about the past and how things could have been different.

Someone else (who is sitting in an air conditioned room) will tell you the climate – hot and humid – makes Southerners talk and walk slower than other Americans. How else can you account for their way of life? he'll ask. So the difference is the slower pace or rhythm of life.

And the fifth person will tell you what makes the South special is the music. Country music has its capital at Opryland in Nashville, Tennessee. Elvis Presley was born in Mississippi, and made his home, called Graceland, in Memphis, Tennessee. Louisiana is the home of Cajun music, ragtime, Dixieland jazz and the blues. Gospels and spirituals got their start on the southern plantations. And if that's not enough, she'll tell you, there's even a distinctive type of good ol' rock 'n' roll called southern rock - ZZ Top, Stevie Ray Vaughan, Lynyrd Skynyrd, etc - not to mention progressive bands such as R.E.M., the B-52's and the many other bands from Athens, Georgia.

So while you are exploring the Southeast, you may want to look beyond the everyday American – and international – businesses such as Coca-Cola, CNN, Compaq Computers or Delta Airlines (which are, by the way, all southern). Listen closely to the music, go outside and experience the weather, visit a history museum and a plantation home. Now you tell me what is special about the South!*

---

14 well-suited *gut geeignet* **15 sugar-cane** *Zuckerrohr* **18 attached** full of affection for **20/21 ever-expanding** always growing larger **23 abolish** to end the existence of a law, an institution, etc **26 struggle** conflict **29 forefather** ancestor; *Vorfahr* **37 humid** *warm und feucht* **39 to account for sth** to explain sth

36  The South

Understanding the text Summarise the five different descriptions in one sentence each.

Discussing the text How do you account for the very different ways in which people describe a region such as the South?

Going beyond the text In groups of five, describe what makes your region of the country different from other regions.

Pre-reading activity Did you know that the first Africans brought to America worked as indentured servants, meaning they were set free after working a set number of years for another person? What do you know about the African slave trade?

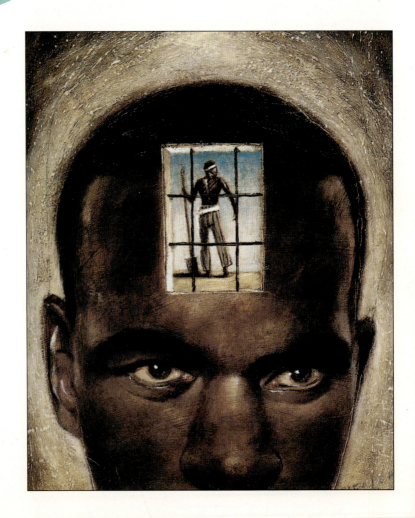

More Than Just A Region

The Primitive

taken from the
shores of Mother Africa.
the savages they thought
we were –
5 they being the real savages.
to save us. (from what?)
our happiness, our love, each other?
their bible for
our land. (introduced to economics)
10 christianized us.
raped our minds with:
T.V. & straight hair,
Reader's Digest & bleaching creams,
tarzan & jungle jim,
15 used cars & used homes,
reefers & napalm,
european history & promises.

Those alien concepts
of whiteness,
20 the being of what
is not.
against our nature,
this weapon called
civilization –
25 they brought us here –
to drive us mad.
(like them)

Don L. Lee

Understanding the poem
1. Who do "we" and "they" refer to?
2. What does the speaker of the poem accuse "them" of?
3. What is the speaker's attitude (feeling) toward his being "civilized"? List the words and phrases which support your answer.

Discussing the poem
1. What does the speaker mean by "raped our minds with ... promises"?
2. Comment on the list of things with which their "minds were raped."
3. How does the title add meaning to the poem?
4. Discuss the picture on page 36 within the context of the poem.

Working with the language
Rephrase the contents of ll. 1-9 with four statements, beginning each with "They ...."

---

2 shore land along the edge of the sea **5 savage** (dated offensive) member of a primitive tribe **11 to rape** vergewaltigen **13 Reader's Digest** very popular monthly magazine containing short reading selections; *Das Beste* **bleaching cream** lotion used to make the skin white or pale **14 jungle jim** (orig Jungle Gym™) *Klettergerüst* **16 reefer** a marijuana cigarette **napalm** ['neɪpɪm] a jelly made from petrol that burns and is used in making bombs, esp in the Vietnam War **18 alien** not familiar; strange **26 to drive sb mad** to make sb mentally ill

 The South

Pre-reading activity The following timeline lists some of the most important dates in early African-American history. Notice how slowly the social situation changed. What caused this slow change?

The Road From Slavery To Freedom

1619 First black bound servants arrive in America. After working a number of years, they are usually freed.

1698 Slave trade opens; slavery is established.

1793 Congress passes Fugitive Slave Law, requiring authorities of all states and territories to arrest and return fugitive slaves.

1795 Dred Scott born a slave in Virginia. Later moves with owners to Missouri, where in 1848 he sues to obtain his freedom because he lives in a free territory. He loses the lawsuit in 1857, but is finally emancipated.

1808 Importation of slaves forbidden by Congress.

1852 Harriet Beecher Stowe publishes *Uncle Tom's Cabin*.

1863 President Lincoln issues the Emancipation Proclamation, freeing Confederate slaves.

1865 Slavery officially prohibited by the 13th Amendment.

1868 All persons born or naturalized in the United States (including slaves) are officially declared U.S. citizens. Voting discrimination based on race, color, or previous condition of servitude is forbidden.

1901 Adoption of poll taxes and "understanding" requirement for prospective voters, which severely limits the black vote.

Going beyond the text Imagine you were born black in Virginia in either 1645, 1745 or 1845. Describe some of the struggles and triumphs you would have experienced within a 60-year life span.

---

bound forced by law, circumstances or duty to do sth **fugitive** trying to avoid being arrested **to sue** to start a legal case in order to make a claim against sb **to obtain** (rather fml) to get sth by making an effort **lawsuit** Prozess **to publish** veröffentlichen **to issue** to make sth known formally **servitude** state of being forced to work for others and having no freedom **poll tax** tax to be paid at the same rate by every adult in a community

Internet Museum of Afro-American History, Boston → http://www.afroammuseum.org/

Booker T. Washington

Booker T. Washington was born into slavery in 1856. After he was freed when he was nine, he began to work in West Virginia. In 1881 he was chosen to be the first principal of the newly established Tuskegee Institute. When he started there, the school consisted of little more than two run-down buildings and 31 uneducated blacks from local farms. When he died 34 years later, Tuskegee had become a respected university with over 100 well-equipped buildings, 1,500 students and nearly 200 faculty members.

Washington urged blacks to accept their inferior social position for the present and to try to improve themselves through vocational training and economic independence. Most blacks agreed with Washington, and for a long time he was the most prominent black man in America. He established the National Negro Business League in 1900, which emphasized skill, thrift and black capitalism. He also wrote a dozen books, including *The Future of the American Negro* (1899), *My Larger Education* (1911) and *Up From Slavery* (1901), from which the following excerpt was taken.

Pre-reading activity

What questions would you like to be able to ask someone who grew up as a slave on a plantation?

Childhood In The Slave Quarters

Booker T. Washington

Of my ancestry I know almost nothing. In the slave quarters, and even later, I heard whispered conversations among the coloured people of the tortures which the slaves, including, no doubt, my ancestors on my mother's side, suffered in the middle passage of the slave ship while being conveyed from Africa to America. I have been unsuccessful in securing any information that would throw any accurate light upon the history of my family beyond my mother. She, I remember, had a half-brother and a half-sister. In the days of slavery not very much attention was given to family history and family records – that is, black family records. My mother, I suppose, attracted the attention of a purchaser who was afterward my owner and hers. Her addition to the slave family attracted about as much attention as the purchase of a new horse or cow. Of my father I know even less than of my mother. I do not even know his name. I have heard reports to the effect that he was a white man who lived on one of the nearby plantations. Whoever he was, I never heard of his taking the least interest in me or providing in any way for my rearing. But I do not find especial fault with him. He was simply another unfortunate victim of the institution which the nation unhappily had engrafted upon it at that time.

The cabin was not only our living-place, but was also used as the kitchen for the plantation. My

---

Tuskegee [tʌsˈkiːgi] **1 ancestry** the group of people or race from which one is descended **2 to whisper** to speak quietly **4 torture** Qual **5 to suffer** to experience sth unpleasant **6 middle passage** the slave trading route across the Atlantic from West Africa to America (here also: the hollow part of the ship where cargo is held) **7 to convey** to carry or transport **8 to secure** (fml) to obtain sth **13 family records** documents about births, marriages, deaths in a family **14 to suppose** to guess **15 purchaser** cf to purchase: to buy **21 to the effect** giving the meaning **24 to provide for sth** (fml) to make it possible for sth to be done later **rearing** cf to rear: to care for young children until they are fully grown **25 to find fault with sb** jdn bemängeln **26 unfortunate** contrary to what one would have liked **27 to engraft upon** aufpfropfen auf; übertragen auf **29 cabin** a small house, usu made of wood

mother was the plantation cook. The cabin was without glass windows; it had only openings in the side which let in the light, and also the cold, chilly air of winter. There was a door to the cabin – that is, something that was called a door – but the uncertain hinges by which it was hung, and the large cracks in it, to say nothing of the fact that it was too small, made the room a very uncomfortable one. In addition to these openings there was, in the lower righthand corner of the room, the "cat-hole," – a contrivance which almost every mansion or cabin in Virginia possessed during the ante-bellum period. The "cat-hole" was a square opening, about seven by eight inches, provided for the purpose of letting the cat pass in and out of the house at will during the night. In the case of our particular cabin I could never understand the necessity for this convenience, since there were at least a half-dozen other places in the cabin that would have accommodated the cats. There was no wooden floor in our cabin, the naked earth being used as a floor. In the centre of the earthen floor there was a large, deep opening covered with boards, which was used as a place in which to store sweet potatoes during the winter. An impression of this potato-hole is very distinctly engraved upon my memory, because I recall that during the process of putting the potatoes in and taking them out I would often come into possession of one or two, which I roasted and thoroughly enjoyed. There was no cooking-stove on our plantation, and all the cooking for the whites and slaves my mother had to do over an open fireplace, mostly in pots and "skillets." While the poorly built cabin caused us to suffer with cold in the winter, the heat from the open fireplace in summer was equally trying.

The early years of my life, which were spent in the little cabin, were not very different from those of thousands of other slaves. My mother, of course, had little time in which to give attention to the training of her children during the day. She snatched a few moments for our care in the early morning before her work began, and at night after the day's work was done. One of my earliest recollections is that of my mother cooking a chicken late at night, and awakening her children for the purpose of feeding them. How or where she got it I do not know. I presume, however, it was procured from our owner's farm. Some people may call this theft. If such a thing were to happen now, I should condemn it as theft myself. But taking place at the time it did, and for the reason that it did, no one could ever make me believe that my mother was guilty

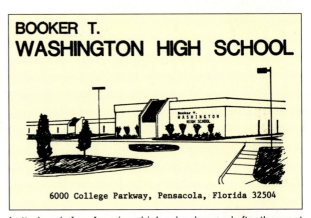

Letterhead of an American high school named after the great black educator.

---

34 chilly rather cold and unpleasant **36 hinge** *Scharnier* **41 contrivance** [aɪ] clever or complicated device or tool, esp one made for a particular purpose **42 mansion** large, impressive house **42/43 to possess** to have or own sth **43 ante-bellum** before the (here: Civil) war **48 necessity** circumstances that force one to do sth **49 convenience** a device that is useful or helpful **51 to accommodate sb** to be helpful to sb **54 earthen** made of earth **55 board** long thin flat piece of wood **59 distinct** clear **to engrave sth on sth** to impress sth deeply on the memory or mind **63 to roast** to cook meat, etc in an oven or over a fire **64 thorough** [ˈθʌrə, US also ˈθʌroʊ] complete **to enjoy sth** *genießen* **69 skillet** frying-pan **72 trying** here: difficult or annoying; hard to deal with **77 training** here: *Erziehung* **78 to snatch** to take sth quickly, esp when a chance to do so occurs **81 recollection** a thing or event that is remembered **82 to awaken** to wake sb up; to make sb stop sleeping **84 to presume** to suppose sth to be true **85 to procure sth** to obtain sth **86 theft** an act or the crime of stealing **87 to condemn** to criticize

More Than Just A Region

of thieving. She was simply a victim of the system of slavery. I cannot remember having slept in a bed until after our family was declared free by the Emancipation Proclamation. Three children – John, my older brother, Amanda, my sister, and myself – had a pallet on the dirt floor, or, to be more correct, we slept in and on a bundle of filthy rags laid upon the dirt floor.

Up From Slavery, 1901

Understanding the text

Give each of the three paragraphs of this text a title. Then summarise the contents of each paragraph in just three or four sentences.

Discussing the text

Which of your questions (from the pre-reading activity) were answered by this article? What would you like to ask him now that you know a little about his childhood in the slave quarters?

Working with the language

Replace the phrases in the following sentences:
l. 6/7 ... while being conveyed ...
l. 8 ... securing any information
l. 9 ... throw any accurate light upon ...
l. 17/18 ... about as much attention as ...
l. 31/32 ... was without ...
l. 46 ... at will ...
l. 60/61 ... during the process of putting in ... and taking out ...
l. 62/63 ... come into possession of ...

Translate

Lines 80–98.

Creative writing

1. Retell *one* of the episodes from the text as if you were the child Booker T. Washington telling a friend about what had happened.
2. Write a similar text, telling the story of what you know about your ancestry, where you grew up and then one childhood memory you remember particularly well. Use some of the same sentence structures and words as are used in the original text.

---

91 to thieve to steal **94 Emancipation Proclamation** public statement made by Pres. Lincoln which freed all the slaves in 1863 **96 pallet** here: a mattress filled with straw **98 filthy** dirty in a disgusting way **rags** piece of old, often torn, cloth

Internet Booker T. Washington High School → http://204.78.125.4/schscnts/wash/btwhome.html

 The South

The Civil War

From Plantation Life To Civil War

The Civil War, the only major war fought on American soil, has a particular hold on the American consciousness. Before the war broke out in 1861, white Southerners had the highest average standard of living in the world. Corn, tobacco, indigo, rice, sugarcane, hemp and cotton were the main crops grown on southern plantations. These large plantations would have been impossible to run without slave labour. From 1619 to 1808 around 650,000 Africans were brought to the United States, mostly to the South. Although only one quarter of all Southerners owned slaves in 1860, the regional economy had grown dependent on the institution.

The growing importance of industry in the North, on the other hand, made slavery less important to the northern economy. Anti-slavery movements began in the early 19th century up north. Although the legal importation of slaves ended in 1808, as required by the Constitution, slavery itself did not. Nineteen states (in the North and West) prohibited slavery by 1861 and 15 (mostly in the South) still permitted it.

Eleven southern states had seceded from the Union by 1861 over the issue of slavery. They feared that President Abraham Lincoln would ban or restrict slavery in the entire nation. (Many Southerners also believed that the powers of the U.S. Government did not supersede the rights of the states.) Realizing the elimination of slavery would threaten their economic survival, they formed the Confederate States of America and became a separate nation. When the Confederacy attacked a U.S. military post in South Carolina, President Lincoln sent troops to recapture the fort. The South saw this as a declaration

Completed in 1922, the Lincoln Memorial in Washington, D.C., was built to honour Abraham Lincoln (1809–1865), the 16th President of the United States. In 1963 – one hundred years after Lincoln issued the Emancipation Proclamation – Martin Luther King Jr gave his famous "I have a dream" speech here.

---

2 soil here: territory **6 hemp** *Hanf* **23 to permit** [-'-] to allow sth **24 to secede (from sth)** to become independent **29 to ban** to forbid **34 to supersede** here: to go over **37 to threaten** [θretn] **46/47 to recapture** to take again sth previously taken by an enemy **47 fort** [fɔːt]

More Than Just A Region

of war. The "War Between the States" had begun.

Four years later a defeated and out-numbered Confederate army surrendered to the Union army. The newest military innovations such as trench warfare, mines, repeating rifles and armoured ships had made this the first "modern" war in history. From 1861-1865, more than 600,000 lives were lost and 470,000 people were wounded. Every third household in the South had lost a son or father. Most of the railroad tracks had been destroyed, and cities such as Atlanta, Columbia, Richmond and Jackson had gone up in flames. The Atlantan newspaper editor Henry Grady wrote that after the war, the Confederate veteran returned to find "his house in ruins, his farm devastated, his slaves free, his stock killed, his barns empty, his trade destroyed, his money worthless." *

Understanding the text

1. Why is the Civil War so important to the history of the United States?
2. In what ways had the North and South grown apart before the war?
3. Describe the effects the war had on the South.

Going beyond the text

Southerners refer to the Civil War as "The War Between the States," "The War of Northern Aggression" or "The Late Unpleasantness" *(Die jüngste Unfreundlichkeit)*. How do these labels convey the southern attitude towards this war?

Pre-reading activity

What do spies do during a war?

The Spy's A Broad

Perhaps the most colorful southern spy during the Civil War was Belle Boyd. Belle's family lived in Martinsburg in what is now West Virginia, where her father was a very successful merchant. She was sent to finishing school in Baltimore at the age of twelve, and returned to Martinsburg a spirited young lady. Belle was only seventeen years of age when the war broke out, but she felt she had to do something to help the South. She decided to try her hand at spying. When her hometown was occupied by Union troops, Belle quickly became known as an out-

---

51 to defeat to win a victory over sb **52 to surrender (to sb)** to stop resisting an enemy **59 to wound** [wuːnd] **66 devastated** ['devəsteɪtɪd] (adj) destroyed completely; ruined **67 stock** here: farm animals **barn** *Scheune*

Internet   Civil War → http://sunsite.utk.edu/civil-war/warweb.html

broad (sl) woman **1 colorful** (Brit colourful) **5 merchant** businessman **finishing school** private school where girls are taught how to behave in fashionable society **7 spirited** lively **10 to try one's hand at sth** to attempt sth for the first time

The South

The White House of the Confederacy in Richmond, VA, former home of President Jefferson Davis

spoken southern firebrand. The rumor that she had Confederate flags plastered all over her bedroom was spread throughout the northern camps. A group of drunken Union soldiers decided to see for themselves if the rumor was true. One day, they demanded entry into the house and threatened to burn it down if they found flags within. Belle and her mother met the soldiers in front of the house and defiantly refused them entry. A quick thinking servant pulled down all the Rebel banners from the bedroom and safely hid them away. The soldiers were outraged at being denied entry and profanely threatened Belle and her mother, at which time Belle produced a revolver and shot one of the Union soldiers. Fearing what would happen next, a Union officer was summoned to the scene and found the conduct of the troops to be against military regulations. The officer placed a guard at the Boyd house to ensure they would not be disturbed again. The posting of this guard gave Belle her first opportunity to gather information for the Confederacy. She flirted and talked with the guards until they were infatuated with her. In the course of conversation she picked up information she felt would be useful to the southern leaders. [...]

Belle was still not a very good spy when it came to keeping her actions inconspicuous. She was reported some thirty times, arrested six and imprisoned on two occasions. The second time she was imprisoned, she had been caught aboard the blockade runner "Greyhound," en route to London where Jefferson Davis had asked her to take some important dispatches. While in prison, she fell in love with her guard, Lieutenant Sam Hardinge. The Lieutenant accompanied her to her trial in Boston, where the romantic nature of her captors allowed her to

---

12/13 outspoken (adj) saying openly exactly what one thinks **13 firebrand** socially or politically active person who is thought by others to cause trouble **rumor** (Brit rumour) story spread by being talked about but may not be true **21 defiant** [dɪˈfaɪənt] openly refusing to obey **25 to outrage** to make sb very shocked, angry or upset **to deny sth (to sb)** to refuse to give sb what they want **25/26 profane** [prəˈfeɪn] not sacred; *grob* **29 to summon** (fml) to send a message telling sb to come **30 conduct** ['--] behaviour **32 to ensure** to make sure of sth; to guarantee sth **37 infatuated** having a very strong passion for sb **41 inconspicuous** [ˌɪnkənˈspɪkjuəs] not very noticeable **45 aboard** on a ship **blockade runner** a ship used to get through a blockade **45/46 en route** [ˌɒn ˈruːt] (French) on the way **46 Jefferson Davis** President of the Confederacy during the Civil War **47 dispatch** official message sent quickly **49 lieutenant** [US luːˈtenənt; Brit lefˈtenənt] **51 nature** here: typical characteristics of a person **captor** person who captures another person

More Than Just A Region

escape to Canada. From there, she set sail again to London, where she was joined shortly by Lt. Hardinge, and the two were married. [...]
55 Belle took to the stage as an actress in London and continued the profession upon her return to America after the war. Her dramatic portrayals of her wartime activities delighted audiences throughout the land. In later years she faced controversy when she was accused of exagger- 60 ating her deeds. The debate about her actions continues today.
Robert P. Broadwater
Daughters of the Cause, 1993

Understanding the text

In what ways was Belle Boyd emancipated?

Creative writing

Write an imaginary dialogue between Belle and one of the drunken Union soldiers who came to her house.

Working with the language

1. List the words used to describe Belle Boyd. Now find some synonyms and antonyms for these words.
2. Find the predicates in the main clauses of the sentences found in lines 18–49. Now write new sentences using these verbs in a new context. Make any passive constructions into active ones.

Reconstruction: Rebuilding The South

Though the victory of the North in the American Civil War assured the integrity of the United States as an indivisible nation, much was destroyed in the course of the conflict, and the
5 secondary goal of the war, the abolition of the system of slavery, was only imperfectly achieved.
The defeat of the Confederacy (Southern states) left what had been the country's most fertile
10 agricultural area economically destroyed and its rich culture devastated. At the same time, the legal abolition of slavery did not ensure equality in fact for former slaves. Immediately after the Civil War, legislatures in the Southern states, fearful of the ways in which former slaves might 15 exercise the right to vote and also eager to salvage what they could of their former way of life, attempted to block blacks from voting. They did this by enacting "black codes" to restrict the freedom of former slaves. Although "radical" 20 Republicans in Congress tried to protect black civil rights and to bring blacks into the main-

52 to set sail to begin a voyage **55 to take to sth** to begin to do sth as a habit **58 to delight** to cause a source of pleasure **59 to face** to be forced to deal with a difficult or unpleasant situation **60 to be accused of sth** *angeklagt* **60/61 to exaggerate** to make sth seem better than it really is **61 deed** act

to reconstruct to build again sth that has been destroyed **2 to assure** to guarantee **integrity** here: the condition of being whole and not divided **3 indivisible** that cannot be divided **5 goal** aim **9 fertile** ['fɜːtaɪl; US 'fɜːrtl] that can produce good crops **10 to destroy** to damage sth so badly that it no longer works **11 to devastate** ['devəsteɪt] to ruin sth **12 abolition** cf to abolish: to end the existence of a law, a practice, an institution **to ensure** to guarantee sth **15 fearful** nervous and afraid **16 eager** full of interest or desire **16/17 to salvage** ['sælvɪdʒ] to save sth from loss **19 to enact** [-'-] to make or pass a law **to restrict** to put a limit on sth **22/23 mainstream** beliefs, attitudes, etc that are shared by most people

The South

Black freedmen proudly voted in state elections under the Reconstruction Plan of 1867.

stream of American life, their efforts were opposed by President Andrew Johnson, a Southerner who had remained loyal to the Union during the Civil War. He served as a Republican vice president, and was elevated to the presidency on the assassination of Abraham Lincoln. [...]

Congress nevertheless was able to press forward with its program of "Reconstruction," or reform, of the Southern states, occupied after the war by the army of the North. By 1870, Southern states were governed by groups of blacks, cooperative whites and transplanted Northerners (called "carpetbaggers"). Many Southern blacks were elected to state legislatures and to the Congress. Although some corruption existed in these "reconstructed" state governments, they did much to improve education, develop social services and protect civil rights.

Reconstruction was bitterly resented by most Southern whites, some of whom formed the Ku Klux Klan, a violent secret society that hoped to protect white interests and advantages by terrorizing blacks and preventing them from making social advances. By 1872, the federal government had suppressed the Klan, but white Democrats continued to use violence and fear to regain control of their state governments. Reconstruction came to an end in 1877, when new constitutions had been ratified in all Southern states and all federal troops were withdrawn from the South.

Despite Constitutional guarantees, Southern blacks were now "second-class citizens" – that is, they were subordinated to whites, though they still had limited civil rights. In some Southern states, blacks could still vote and hold elective office. There was racial segregation in schools and hospitals, but trains, parks and other

Tenant farmers remained dependent on the landlord for their survival.

---

23 effort ['--] an attempt or an action directed towards a particular cause **24 to oppose** to express strong disagreement with sth **27 to elevate** to raise sb to a higher place or rank **30/31 to press forward with sth** to continue doing sth in a determined way **37/38 carpetbagger** *politischer Abenteurer, der mit nichts als einer Reisetasche nach dem Sezessionskrieg in die besetzten Südstaaten kam* **50 to resent** [-'-] to feel bitter or angry about sth offensive, etc **61 to suppress** to put an end to sth esp by force **65 to regain** to get sth back again after losing it **67 to ratify** (fml) to make an agreement officially valid, usu by signing it **68 to withdraw (from sth)** to go back or away from a place **72 to subordinate** to treat sth or sb as of lesser importance than sth or sb else **landlord** person, esp a man, from whom one rents land

More Than Just A Region

public facilities could still generally be used by people of both races.

Toward the end of the century, this system of segregation and oppression of blacks grew far more rigid. In the 1896 case of *Plessy v. Ferguson,* the United States Supreme Court ruled that the Constitution permitted separate facilities and services for the two races, so long as these facilities and services were equal. Southern state legislatures promptly set aside separate – but unequal – facilities for blacks. Laws enforced strict segregation in public transportation, theaters, sports, and even elevators and cemeteries. Most blacks and many poor whites lost the right to vote because of their inability to pay the poll taxes (which had been enacted to exclude them from political participation) and their failure to pass literacy tests. Blacks accused of minor crimes were sentenced to hard labor, and mob violence was sometimes perpetrated against them. Most Southern blacks, as a result of poverty and ignorance, continued to work as tenant farmers. Although blacks were legally free, they still lived and were treated very much like slaves.

Jonathan Rose

U.S. Information Agency, 1986

Understanding the text

1. Make a list of the things that changed in the United States after the Civil War was over.
2. What were the aims of the congressional Reconstruction plan and how long did this period last?
3. To what extent did the plan (not) reach its aims?

Translate

Lines 1–7 and lines 30–48.

Civil Rights

From Freedom To Civil Rights

The Civil Rights Movement in the United States included the political, legal, and social struggle by black Americans to gain full citizenship rights and to achieve racial equality. The Civil Rights Movement was mainly a challenge to segregation, the system of laws and customs separating blacks and whites that whites used to control blacks after slavery was abolished in the 1860s. During the Civil Rights Movement, individuals and civil

---

88 to enforce to make sure that a law is obeyed **92 poll tax** tax to be paid at the same rate by every adult in a community **94 literacy test** ['lɪtərəsi] (also known as an "understanding" test) test to show if sb is able to read and write **96 labor** (Brit labour) **mob** large crowd of people **97 to perpetrate** ['pɜːpətreɪt] (fml) to commit a crime **100 tenant farmer** ['tenənt] (also known as "sharecroppers") person who pays rent to a landlord for the use of land

Internet   U.S. Information Agency → http://www.usia.gov/usis.html

struggle conflict **citizenship rights** Bürgerrechte **challenge (to sth)** statement or action that questions or disputes sth

rights organizations challenged segregation and discrimination with a variety of activities, including protest marches, boycotts, and refusal to abide by segregation laws. Many believe that the movement began with the Montgomery bus boycott in 1955 and ended with the Voting Rights Act of 1965, though there is debate about when it began and whether it has ended yet.

1909 National Association for the Advancement of Colored People (NAACP) is founded.

1948 President Truman issues an order ending segregation in the military.

1954 U.S. Supreme Court in *Brown versus Board of Education* declares school segregation unconstitutional.

1955 Rosa Parks, a black woman, refuses to give up her seat on a bus to a white man. This sparks off the Civil Rights Movement with a year-long boycott of buses in Montgomery, Alabama.

1957 Little Rock, Arkansas: The first nine black students are placed in Central High School but prevented from attending classes by angry white mobs. President Eisenhower sends in federal troops to escort the students to school.

1960 Lunch counter confrontations: Non-violent sit-ins of segregated lunch counters and other areas are undertaken by the Student Nonviolent Coordination Committee (SNCC) following Gandhian principles.

1961 Groups of "Freedom Riders" (black and white members and supporters of the Congress of Racial Equality) challenge segregation practices throughout the South by sitting in "white only" seats on public transport.

1963 James Meredith becomes the first black student to be registered at the University of Mississippi, but only after federal intervention from President Kennedy.

March on Washington: 200,000 blacks and whites gather in Washington. Martin Luther King Jr gives one of the most famous speeches of the Civil Rights Movement: "I have a dream ...."

1964 Civil Rights Act of 1964 prohibits discrimination in public accommodations (public housing, hospitals, etc.), in education and employment.

1965 Voting Rights Act. Like the Civil Rights Act, it attempts to do away with Jim Crow laws. Leads to drastic increases in the numbers of black registered voters in the South and a comparable increase in the number of blacks holding elective offices there.

1971 Decision on school busing: Desegregation is constitutional when ordered by courts (applied to busing of students from home to the school of their choice).

1972 Equal Opportunity and Employment Act: People from ethnic minorities are to be preferred in the promotion and hir-

---

refusal cf to refuse: to say or show that one is unwilling to give, accept or do sth **to abide by sth** to accept and act according to a law **advancement** process of helping sth to make progress or succeed **colored** (Brit coloured; dated, often offensive) of a race that does not have a white skin **to issue** to make sth known formally **segregation** cf to segregate: to separate a group of people from the rest of the community, esp because of their race, and treat them differently **Supreme Court** the highest court in the USA **to spark sth off** to be the immediate cause of sth **to prevent** to hinder **counter** long flat table where customers are served **to challenge** to question whether sth is right **act** here: law **comparable** ['kɒmpərəbl]

ing of personnel for jobs. "Affirmative action" means setting aside a certain proportion of jobs for ethnic minorities, even though they may not be as qualified as white males.

1983 President Reagan signs legislation designating Martin Luther King Jr's birthday a national holiday.

1989 L. Douglas Wilder becomes Virginia's and the nation's first elected black governor.

1992 Rodney King is beaten by four policemen in Los Angeles. The action, privately videotaped and shown on national TV, sparks off riots which leaves 53 dead.

1994 O. J. Simpson, a black American football hero, is accused of having murdered his ex-wife and her friend. The long, nationally televised trial intensifies tensions between blacks and whites. Simpson is found not guilty in 1995 in the criminal trial, yet is pronounced guilty in 1997 in the civil trial and is ordered to pay a total of $33.5 million in damages to the victims' families.

1995 The Million Man March, organized by militant black leader Louis Farrakhan, draws nearly 400,000 black men to Washington, D.C., in order to give them a renewed commitment to their personal improvement, their families and their black communities.

Understanding the text

To what extent has the movement from freedom to civil rights been peaceful?

Going beyond the text

1. Based on the information given in the timeline, guess when this picture was taken.
2. Imagine how race relations may develop in the USA.

---

personnel [--'-] **legislation** law or series of laws

(Internet) National Civil Rights Museum, Memphis, TN → http://www.mecca.org/~crights

(Internet) Afro-America → http://www.afroam.org/

 The South

Martin Luther King Jr: The Man And His Message

Martin Luther King Jr was born in Atlanta on Jan. 15, 1927, the son of a Baptist minister. He himself also became a minister when he was 18. He gained national attention as leader of the 1955 bus boycott in Montgomery, Alabama. He was one of the organizers of the large (200,000 people) march on Washington, D.C., in 1963 to demand racial equality. This was where he made his famous "I have a dream" speech. An advocate of non-violence, he was awarded the Nobel Peace Prize in 1964. He was shot and killed in Memphis, Tennessee, by James Earl Ray on April 4, 1968.

"We cannot solve this problem through retaliatory violence. We must meet violence with non-violence."

"Let us march on segregated housing!
Let us march on segregated schools!
Let us march on poverty!
Let us march on ballot boxes!"

"We must learn to live together as brothers or perish together as fools."

"I want to be the white man's brother, not his brother-in-law."

"Injustice anywhere is a threat to justice everywhere."

"I submit to you that if a man hasn't discovered something he will die for, he isn't fit to live."

"I have a dream that my four little children will one day live in a nation where they will not be judged by the color of their skin but by the content of their character."

"The means by which we live have outdistanced the ends for which we live. Our scientific power has outrun our spiritual power. We have guided missiles and misguided men."

Understanding the texts — What do these excerpts tell you about Martin Luther King Jr and his mission?

Analysing the texts — What stylistic devices does Martin Luther King Jr use in these excerpts?

---

perish ['periʃ] to die **brother-in-law** [lɔː] the brother of one's husband or wife **injustice** [-'--] an unfair act **threat** [θret] possibility of trouble, danger or ruin **to submit** to give sth to sb so that it may be formally considered **to be fit to do sth** suitable and right by normal social standards **to judge** to form an opinion about sb/sth; to estimate the value of sth **content** ['--] the amount of sth contained in sth else **retaliatory** [rɪ'tæliətri; US -,tɔːri] cf to retaliate to fight back **means** Mittel **to outdistance** to move faster than and leave behind **ends** Ziel, Zweck **to outrun** to develop faster than sth **guided missiles** ['mɪsaɪl; US 'mɪsl] rocket which can be led to its destination while in flight by electronic devices **misguided** [,mɪs'gaɪdɪd] wrong because of having or showing bad judgement **ballot box** box for votes

Internet Martin Luther King Jr → http://www.blackvoices.com/feature/mlk_98/index.html

More Than Just A Region

Black Migration From The South 1940–1970

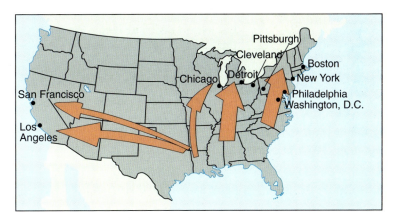

Between 1940 and 1970 more than 5 million African-Americans, thrown out of work by mechanical cotton pickers and excluded by Jim Crow laws, left the old Confederacy – the largest internal ethnic migration in American history. Since 1975, however, middle-class African-Americans have been returning to their roots in great numbers. If the trend continues, by 2010 around 2.7 million will have returned.

Going Back Home

Sometimes I wonder   why did I ever leave home
Sometimes I wonder   why'd I ever leave home

I had a few dollars in my pocket
Ooh now that little change is gone

5 I didn't think a city   Whoa could be so doggone mean
I didn't think a city   Boy could be so doggone mean

---

4 change here: *Kleingeld* **5 doggone** [ˈdɒgɒn; US ˈdɔːgɔːn] (US infml) (used to express annoyance or surprise)

 The South

Ah but this is the meanest place   hahaha
Lord I've ever seen

I used to have a job   doing spot labor every day
10 I used to have a job   doing spot labor everyday

But when I got to work this morning
Lord they'd packed up and move away

I called my boss   Well I want to know can I come back home
Yes, I called my boss   I want to know can I come back home

15 He said Nah, you know sorry Son, haha
Boy your house is gone

Mmmmhmm   What in the world am I going to do
Mmmmhmm   Where in the world am I gonna be

I guess it's just all wrapped up in a nutshell now
20 Oh it look like old pro Son is through

Son Seals

Understanding the song

Tell the singer's story in your own words.

Discussing the song

1. Why are some lines or phrases repeated? What effect does this repetition have?
2. Look at the map and text above and comment on them after having read the song.

You Stand Accused Of Being Black

Mildred D. Taylor

For the Logan children, growing up black in Mississippi is a slow awakening to the reality of poverty and racism as it exists during the Depression years. Whereas the Logans have succeeded in avoiding serious trouble, another young friend, T.J. Avery, has not been so fortunate. T.J. is standing trial, accused of murdering a white storekeeper.

Mr. Jamison walked the length of the jury box looking at each juror in turn. "T.J. Avery has confessed to what he has done. But I ask each of you, what really is his crime? He followed two white men blindly. They told him to break 5 into the Mercantile and he did as he was told. Now whose fault is that? Haven't we always demanded that Negroes do as they are told?

---

9 spot labor (Brit labour) little jobs usually paid by the day **19 in a nutshell** in aller Kürze **20 through** here: finished

Depression years the worst years of the recession from 1929 to the late 1930s **to stand trial** to be accused of a crime in a court of law **1 jury box** separate place for the jury (usu twelve persons known as jurors) **6 Mercantile** ['mɜːkəntaɪl; US also -tiːl, -tɪl] here: name of a shop

Haven't we always demanded their obedience?" He waited as if for an answer before going on. "If we teach them to follow us in what we deem is good, isn't it logical that they should follow our lead into what is not good? We demand they follow us docilely, and if they should dare to disobey, we punish them for their disobedience, as Melvin and R.W. punished T.J. by beating him. T.J. murdered no one. His guilt lies more in his gullibility, in his belief that two white men cared about him, than in anything else.

"If you are asking yourselves, did the Simmses actually play a part in all of this, ask yourselves: Why would T.J. lie about it? He is a black boy. The men of this jury are white. The man who was killed was white. Why would T.J. accuse white men of being part of the break-in that night, of being the actual murderers, when this very accusation could turn you against him? Why? Because, gentlemen, it is the truth." He searched their faces and repeated, "It is the truth ...."

Mr. Macabee's plea to the jury demanded that they remember that the murder of a fine, upstanding citizen had been committed and that that, above all else, had to be the deciding factor, not the age of the defendant, the color of his skin, or the color of the man, murdered. He said all that and the jury heard all that, but I didn't believe for one minute that he believed it or the jury did. But they nodded and left to cast their votes.

The spectators stood and stretched. Some left the courtroom and came outside; most stayed, waiting. The boys and I joined the people on the ground and stood near the old man still sitting at the foot of the tree, None of us said anything as we avoided looking at each other, afraid our fear would be seen, until Christopher-John adamantly declared: "But T.J. ain't killed nobody! He ain't!" Stacey put his hand on Christopher-John's neck and brought him near, but said nothing. There was nothing to say now.

"Well, what did you think of that nigger's story in there?"

We looked around. A group of white farmers stood nearby dividing a chaw of tobacco.

"Aw, it's just nigger talk," scoffed one of them. "Like R.W. said, the nigger was lying." […]

We did not have to wait long. In less than thirty minutes the jury returned. The vote poll was taken. Twelve men in the jury. Twelve votes of guilty. There was to be no mercy. T.J. received the death penalty.

Let the Circle Be Unbroken, 1981

Understanding the text
1. What are Mr. Jamison's arguments to convince the jury of T.J.'s innocence?
2. What arguments does Mr. Macabee put forward?
3. How do the two groups of spectators (the Logan children and the white farmers) react to the trial?

Going beyond the text
Why could there have been no mercy for T. J.?

Working with the language
Put the first part of Mr. Jamison's plea into reported speech (lines 2–20).

9/10 obedience the act of doing what one is told (adj: obedient, verb: to obey) **12 to deem** to judge **14 docile** ['dəʊsaɪl; US 'dɒsl] obedient **18 gullibility** [ˌgʌlə'bɪləti] *Leichtgläubigkeit* **31 plea** [pliː] here: lawyer's argument in court **33 upstanding** important **35 defendant** person accused of a crime **48 adamant** ['---] firm **ain't** (non-standard) here: hasn't **55 chaw** a chew, esp. of tobacco **56 to scoff** to mock and make fun **59 vote poll** here: decision **61 mercy** forgiveness, pity **62 penalty** punishment

 The South

A Taste Of The South

Pre-reading activity Find New Orleans on the map. What importance might a city's location have for its people, its history and development and its commerce?

Ol' Man River Tells His Tale

Well, you know, before the European Americans started moving out to the Louisiana Territory at the beginning of the nineteenth century, I was mostly alone with the natives. They liked
5 the climate and the fact that they could fish from my waters and hunt wildlife on my banks. That all changed in 1812, though. That's when steamboats started traveling up and down me, bringing hides, grain, timber and settlers from the hinterland to the growing town of New 10 Orleans.
Now, it was named *New* Orleans by all the French people who settled here. I guess there must be an *Old* Orleans somewhere in France. They came down from French Canada and 15 named this area Louisiana after their King Louis XIV. But thousands of others came in the early – and mid – 1800s to get in on the good

---

4 native *Ureinwohner* **6 bank** here: land along each side of a river **8 steamboats** *Dampfschiff* **9 hide** animal's skin **grain** *Getreide* **timber** wood prepared for use in building

Internet Cajun and Creole Culture → http://www.cajunculture.com/
Internet New Orleans → http://usacitylink.com/new-orleans/

times of this booming town. Then came the Civil War – which some Southerners still call "The War of Northern Aggression." Most people think all the fighting took place in the East, but there were also battles out here. One of the most decisive Union successes was when Admiral Farragut – a Virginian fighting for the Union! – captured New Orleans, so the Confederates couldn't use me as a trade route any more. After the War ended in 1865 things didn't get much better for poor ol' New Orleans. Most of the beautiful gardens and fine homes got all weed-grown and neglected. Who could afford to keep 'em up? It wasn't until after another war – the Second World War – that trade and industry started to prosper again. They have a song down here called "When the saints come marchin' in." I guess that's what happened.

If you look at the city today, you'll see boatloads of tourists who come to see the lacy grillwork of cast-iron balconies that we call "galleries." With all those French people settling here early on, the city took on a lot of French style. They've been celebrating Mardi Gras (that's French for "fat Tuesday," the day before Ash Wednesday) every spring since about 1820. And you can eat food and hear music influenced by the Cajuns – that's what the Arcadians are called who came down from Canada in the early days.

There's also an obvious amount of Spanish and Caribbean influence in the lifestyle here, from the architecture to the religion. But of the 500,000 inhabitants in New Orleans today, most of them are either wealthy whites or poor blacks. The blacks have certainly had an important impact on the city. I mean, what would it be without their music – jazz? Some say it's a combination of African rhythms and harmonies, plantation music such as spirituals and blues, and other influences such as ragtime and American folk songs. Put all that together and you're bound to get some great sounding music! Never heard of Scott Joplin or Louis Armstrong? I suggest you go listen to some of their music and you'll understand what I'm talking about. They were two of the many successful blacks to come from New Orleans.

Today the city's population is about 62 percent black and many of them are poor. Poverty often leads to crime, but political and religious organizations are starting urban improvement projects. No one would say it's the safest city in the United States, but it surely is one of the liveliest and most colorful!*

The galleries show architectural influences of the French and Spanish styles.

---

28 battle a fight between armies, navies, etc **29 decisive** [dɪˈsaɪsɪv] *entscheidend* **33 to capture** to take control of sth by force **36 trade route** *Handelsweg* **41 weed-grown** *unkrautbewachsen* **to neglect** to give no or not enough care to sth **42 to afford** to have enough money, time, etc for a particular purpose **44 to prosper** to be successful **48 boatload** full amount a boat can carry **49 lacy** *spitzenartig* **grillwork** *Gitter* **50 cast-iron** [ˈaɪən; US ˈaɪərn] *Gusseisen* **65 impact** (on sth) strong impression or effect on sth **71 to be bound to do sth** to be certain to do sth **78 poverty** state of being poor

 The South

Understanding the text

1. Who is the narrator in this text? What is the narrator's relationship to New Orleans?
2. Which cultural influences can one see in New Orleans today?
3. What factors led to New Orleans' rapid growth?
4. What led to its decline?

Going beyond the text

Use your library or the Internet addresses listed on p. 54 to find more information on New Orleans. If you were planning a trip there, what would you want to see or do?

River Riddles

Why does a river sleep a lot?
What part of a river is always up-to-date?
Where do you feed a river?
Why does a river have a lot of money?
5 Why does the water in a river get tired?
Why do some rivers bounce?
Where does the water in a river have the biggest drops?
What part of a river is a Greek letter?
What parts of a river are the fastest?

English Teaching Forum, Vol. XXIX, No. 1, Jan. 1991

A stern-wheeler leaves New Orleans full of passengers for a tour of the lower Mississippi River.

More Than Just A Region 57

As you travel down the river from north to south, how many of the following items can you collect?

1. Title or address for an unmarried woman
2. Third note of the musical scale
3. First person
4. "Yes" in Italian and Spanish
5. A female relative (informal)
6. Exists
7. A small taste of water
8. 3.1416
9. Smallest state of the U.S. (abbr.)
10. Four in ancient Rome
11. Common contraction
12. State in New England (abbr.)
13. British monarch

MISSISSIPPI RIVER

Going upriver is harder. Can you find these?

1. A short word meaning "about" or "concerning"
2. 10–4 in ancient Rome
3. Tear
4. The ratio of the circumference of a circle to its diameter
5. Ninth letter
6. "Yes" in Portuguese
7. A common contraction

Singing These Old Lonesome Blues

Julius Lester

He would never forget the night when he really became a blues singer. He had gone to bed with his mother as usual, but when she was asleep, he slipped outside. He walked a ways from the house so his playing wouldn't wake her. He had been playing different runs he knew on the instrument, not playing any song in particular, when he heard himself begin to sing: "Oh, look at the moon, shining down on me." He heard the guitar repeat the last notes of the line. "Oh, look at the moon, shining down on me." He sang again. The guitar repeated the last notes again. "Sitting here in the cottonfield down in Mississippi." He wondered where the words had come from. He hadn't thought of them. His mouth had simply opened and out had come the blues. "I'm

---

ratio Verhältnis **circumference** Umfang **6 run** Laut

sitting down here," the words came, "singing these old lonesome blues." The guitar said it in its way. "I'm sitting down here," he sang again, but this time the guitar completed the line by itself. "I ain't got nothing, not even a pair of shoes." Then he'd let the guitar talk for a while. It was as if his fingers had a life all their own, moving over the strings without him telling them what strings to pick. Then he heard himself singing, "I wonder sometimes if the moon ever gets the blues. Yes, I wonder sometimes if the moon ever gets the blues. I wonder sometimes if white folk ever lose."

After that the blues had never left him any peace. The words and the music were always there, ready to come out of him whenever he opened his mouth.

"Satan on my track," Long Journey Home

Understanding the text

1. What do you learn of the singer's life?
2. Where does the singer get his inspiration from?

Going beyond the text

Read out the lines which make up the song. Using these lines as a source, describe what blues is.
See "Going Back Home," pp. 51–52, for an example of a blues.

Working with the language

1. "Then he'd let the guitar talk for a while." Give the full form of the verb. Explain your choice.
2. "... without him telling them …"
Use the following prepositions in similar constructions: "with," "through," "by," "before," "after."

Jazz And Jazzmen

[Jazz] is a mixture of rhythms from West Africa, harmony from European classical music, religious music (including gospel songs and negro and white spirituals), work songs, and American folk music. It began as a simple form of folk music and has developed in a number of quite sophisticated ways.

The first organized music to become a part of jazz was ragtime, an energetic style of piano playing with distinctive rhythms. Scott Joplin (whose compositions enjoyed a revival in the 1970s) was the best-known ragtime composer. Ragtime bands also played the blues. [...] Early jazz included a "blue note" – certain notes of the scale that were purposely played slightly flat, giving the music a mournful sound.

Between 1910 and 1920 jazz moved northward, both as a result of the movement of jazz musi-

---

3 gospel songs religious songs based on Bible stories **4 spirituals** songs expressing Christian beliefs **7 sophisticated** refined, complex **10 Scott Joplin** (1868–1917) **11 revival** comeback **15 scale** Tonleiter **purposely** on purpose; *absichtlich* **16 mournful** extremely sad

cians from the South to northern cities such as Chicago and New York and through the music of jazz bands playing on riverboats that made trips up and down the Mississippi River. During the "golden age" of jazz in the 1920s, jazz music flourished throughout the United States.

Louis Armstrong, an outstanding cornet player, became the first well-known male jazz singer, and the first to use scat singing – singing meaningless syllables in place of words. Duke Ellington became known for his contributions as a jazz pianist, songwriter and band leader. In 1932, a song Ellington composed and recorded, called "It Don't Mean a Thing If It Ain't Got That Swing," introduced swing music, played with a happy, relaxed jazz beat. Clarinetist and band leader Benny Goodman became the "king of swing" in 1935, and swing music flourished for the next decade.

"All that Jazz" by Stuart White

English Teaching Forum, Vol. XXIX, No. 1, Jan. 1991

Understanding the text
1. What is the origin of jazz?
2. Explain: ragtime, blues, scat singing and swing music.

Going beyond the text
What kind of music do you like listening to?

---

29 to flourish to grow and spread **31 Louis Armstrong** (1900–1971) **32 cornet** trumpet **38 Duke Ellington** (1899–1974) **49 decade** period of ten years

Internet   Jazz → http://www.allaboutjazz.com

The South

Iced Tea: The Champagne Of The South

When you visit the South, you'll most certainly drink "tea," meaning iced tea. It's served generously
5 over crushed ice in everything from Mason canning jars to fine glassware – refills encouraged. It usually comes
10 presweetened, very presweetened, so if you like yours plain or moderately sugared, you'll need to say so.

To get as fine a brew at home as you can get in the South, follow these simple steps. Bring a
15 quart of fresh cold water to a boil. Pour it over 4

to 6 tea bags (use your favorite) in a heavy, heat-resistant glass or plastic 2-quart container. Let the tea bags steep 5 to 7 minutes, then remove. Add a quart of cold water and some ice, and sugar if you want 20 to presweeten. Let the tea cool to room temperature before refrigerating it – this guarantees that it will remain crystal clear for at least a day. After a day, it will begin to cloud up and acquire a bitter taste. 25
Serve with lemon slices.
For mint iced tea (another Southern treat), add fresh mint leaves while the tea is still hot, and garnish glasses with a sprig of mint, too.
Sheila Lukins   USA Cookbook

Going beyond the text Make your own iced tea according to this recipe. Compare yours to the iced tea you can buy in cartons.

Working with the language Complete the following chart (---- means there is no corresponding part of speech for this word).

noun	verb	adjective	adverb
ice	?	?	?
?	----	?	generously
?	?	canning	----
?	crush	?	----
?	?	sweet	?
?	?	?	moderately
sugar	?	?	----
?	refrigerate	?	----
?	?	cloudy	?
slice	?	?	----

Working with thematic vocabulary Working in groups, choose one of the following topics: the issue of slavery in the South, the Civil War, the Civil Rights Movement or southern culture. Collect words from the texts you have read in this chapter which deal with your chosen topic. Now use 10 of these words in informative sentences about the South.

---

4 generous in large amounts **5 to crush** to break sth hard into small pieces by pressing **6/7 Mason canning jar** *Einmachglas* **8 refill** (infml) another drink of the same type **8/9 to encourage** [-ʹ--] to stimulate sth **10 to presweeten** [-ʹ--] to add sugar before serving **15 quart** [kwɔːt] 1.14 litres in Britain and 0.94 of a litre in the US **16 favorite** (Brit *favourite*) **17 heat-resistant** *hitzebeständig* **18 to steep** *ziehen lassen* **29 to garnish** to decorate food with small additional amounts of food **sprig** small stem with leaves on it taken from a plant

The Southwest: Home To Many Cultures

Top left: A young cowgirl on ranch land in New Mexico. Above left: Navaho girl in Monument Valley. Center: A Mexican-American woman harvesting chilis in New Mexico. Above right: White water rafters on the Colorado River in the Grand Canyon.

The Southwest

Getting to know the Southwest

Make a mind map of what you know about the Southwest.

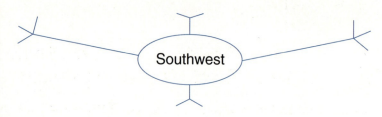

Read the short text below. You may find some more information to help you with your mind map.

Endless Horizons

After spending time in the American Southwest, most other places will seem cramped. This is a land of endless horizons and big skies. At the same time, usually hidden in the land-
5 scape and discovered off the beaten track, are lush green canyons and valleys that rest the eye and provide shelter from the sun. These unexpected pleasures are as much a part of the Southwest as the great masses of red rock and
10 open stretches of desert.

The geographical parameters of the Southwest have been defined in dozens of ways, and sometimes include areas as far east as Oklahoma and Texas; as far west as Southern California and as far north as Salt Lake City, Utah and Reno, 15 Nevada.

Insight Guides, American Southwest

---

2 cramped limited in space **5 off the beaten track** in a place that is far away from other people, houses, etc **6 lush** growing thickly and strongly **to rest the eye** to be pleasing to the eye **7 to provide** to supply, to offer **10 stretch** here: area **11 parameter** [-'---] factor that limits the way in which sth can be done

Home To Many Cultures

> **While-reading activity**
> While you are reading the text, take notes on the important facts.

The People Of The Southwest: Their Past And Present

The first people in the region were the ancestors of today's Native Americans. Archaeologists have excavated fragments of their villages, hunting sites and irrigation ditches, and have
5 found petroglyphs and pictographs – many of which can be seen in protected national monuments and in museums. Today's Southwestern tribes – the Navajo, Apache, Pueblo and Tohono O'odham, among others – relate oral history
10 that shed light on their ancestors and their vibrant cultures and languages reveal traces of their forebears.

The first Europeans in the region were Spanish conquistadors and missionaries, searching for
15 gold, land, slaves and converts. But the Indian tribes had no gold and held land communally. They rebelled against forced labor and resented the new religion. After centuries of overt and covert resistance, many tribes succeeded in
20 maintaining their own cultural identity, and learned the lessons they would rely on when they confronted the next wave of newcomers – the Anglo Americans.

After Mexico won its independence from Spain
25 in 1821, the USA was quick to fight for the new territory. After the Mexican-American War of 1846 to 1847, the USA assumed control over what was to be called the New Mexico Territory, including most of Arizona and New Mexico. Traders continued to travel west from Missouri 30 to New Mexico along the Santa Fe Trail, but the best route to California lay south of the territorial border. In 1853 the Gadsden Purchase brought (what is now called) southern Arizona into US hands. The government soon sent 35 troops to 'clear' the lands of the Native Americans, establishing massive reservations that cover large parts of the Southwest. This was known as the "Long Walk." […]

These three cultures – the Native American, 40 Hispanic and the Anglo American – live side by side today, and while the three have assimilated aspects of each other's cultures, they remain distinct. The large cities of Phoenix, Tucson, Santa Fe and Albuquerque all have districts 45 where one culture or another is more prevalent, and many smaller towns still reflect the ethnicity of their founders in their residents and architecture.

Rob Rachowiecki
Southwest, Lonely Planet Travel Survival Kit, 1995

---

1 ancestor ['ænsestə(r)] person from whom one is descended **2 archaeologist** [ˌɑːkiˈɒlədʒɪst] **3 to excavate** ['ekskəveɪt] to uncover by digging **4 site** certain place **irrigation ditches** system of small canals to supply land or crops with water **5 petroglyph** ancient rock carving **pictograph** ancient or prehistoric drawing or painting on a rock wall **9 to relate** to tell a story **11 vibrant** [aɪ] lively **to reveal** to make known, to show **12 forebear** ancestor **14 conquistador** Spanish for conqueror, person who takes possession and control of a country **15 convert** [ˈ--] person who has changed from one religion, faith, opinion etc to another **17 to resent** [rɪˈzent] to feel, to express, or show anger because of sth **18 overt** [əʊˈvɜːt] not secret **19 covert** secret **20 to maintain** to keep **27 to assume control** to take over **31 Santa Fe Trail** pioneer route to the Southwest used esp 1821–1880 from Kansas City, MO, to Santa Fe, NM **33 Gadsden Purchase** land south of the Gila River in present Arizona and New Mexico purchased 1853 by the United States from Mexico **42 to assimilate** here: to absorb **44 distinct** separate **46 prevalent** ['---] widespread **47/48 ethnicity** [-ˈ---] cultural, religious, linguistic characteristics of a race or group of people

64  The Southwest

Understanding the text Work in groups and use your notes to make a timeline of the main historical facts.

Going beyond the text
1. Look up additional information in your history book or an encyclopedia and include it in your timeline.
2. What important aspects of the Native Americans' life in the Southwest does this petroglyph reflect?

This petroglyph is a very fine example of the Southwest's prehistoric culture.

Working with the language Write down all the words and phrases connected with the word field "history," and add other words you know which relate to history.

Creative writing Write an article about the history of your hometown.

Translate Lines 24–49.

Home To Many Cultures

Exploring The Navajo Nation

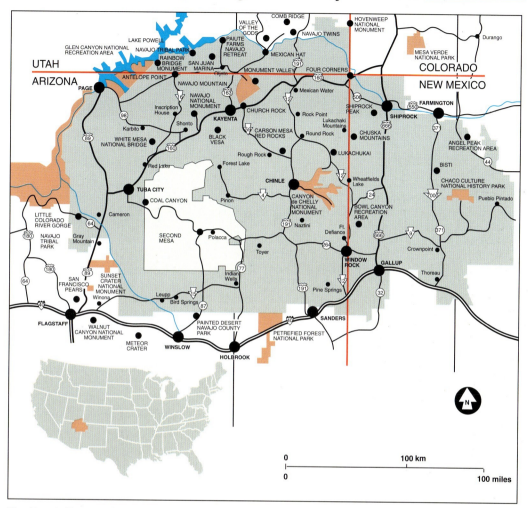

The Navajo Reservation

Tenacious ... adaptable ... enduring ... spiritual – words that characterize the largest and most influential Indian tribe in North America ... The Navajo Nation. Since the Long Walk in the 1860s, the Navajo Nation was decimated to a population of only 8,000. It has increased to a stronghold of more than 210,000. About 60 percent of Navajos are 24 years old or younger. In its infancy, the Navajo Nation governed itself by a complex language and clan system. The discovery of oil in the early 1920s clarified the need for a more systematic form of government. So, in 1923, the Navajos established a tribal government; thus providing an entity to deal

---

Navajo [ˈnævəhəʊ] **1 tenacious** [təˈneɪʃəs] keeping a firm hold on sth **adaptable** [-ˈ---] able to become adjusted to new conditions **enduring** lasting for a long time **7 stronghold** place dominated by a particular group **9 infancy** [ˈɪnfənsi] early stage of the development of sth **11 to clarify** to make obvious **14 to provide** to supply **entity** [ˈ---] institution

The Southwest

New Mexico

Farmington – The Navajo Agricultural Products Industry expects to build a french fry factory next fall that would churn out 300 million pounds of fries and tater tots a year by '00.
USA Today, Dec. 31, 1997

A Navajo elder preparing to do her daily chores.

15 with American oil companies wishing to lease Navajoland for exploration.
Today, the Navajo Tribal Council has grown into the largest and most sophisticated American Indian government in the U.S. It embodies
20 an elected tribal chairman, vice-chairman and 88 council delegates representing 109 local units of government throughout the Navajo Nation.
25 Council delegates meet a minimum of four times a year as a full body in Window Rock, Arizona, the Na-
30 vajo Nation capital. The Navajo Nation continues to forge ahead in its goal to attain economic self-sufficiency. Yet in the midst of it all, the Dineh (or The People) still adhere to their cultural, social and traditional 35 values, the same tenacious values that have made the Navajo Nation unique and fascinating throughout its history. The traditional history of the Navajo Nation, with its strong emphasis on adapting trends with modern day America will 40 continue to perpetuate the enduring Navajo into the future.

Explore the Navajo Nation (brochure)

Navajo jewelry

Understanding the text

1. What do the Navajos want the reader to know about typical characteristics of the Navajo Nation, their history, Navajo politics and economy?
Make a list of key words for each point.

The Navajo Nation's

| characteristics | history | politics | economy |

2. Compare in a class discussion what you used to think about the American Indians with what you now know about the Navajos.

---

16 exploration here: search for natural resources **18 sophisticated** here: advanced **19 to embody** to include **32 to forge ahead** [fɔːdʒ] to advance quickly **33 to attain** to achieve **self-sufficiency** state of supplying all needs without help **35 to adhere to sth** [əd'hɪə(r)] to follow a set of principles, course of action, etc **41 to perpetuate** [pə'petʃueɪt] to make sth continue **chore** task done as part of a routine

Home To Many Cultures

Working with the language

Find the corresponding adjectives, verbs or nouns for the following words: influential, population, government, exploration, elected, emphasis.

noun	verb	adjective
endurance	to endure	enduring
???	???	influential

Visit To A Navajo Park

Navajo Nation Parks Rules & Regulations

1. Respect the privacy and customs of the Navajo people. Enter homes only upon invitation.
2. Please keep Navajoland clean. Do not litter! Do not burn or bury trash. Please place all refuse in trash containers.
3. Alcoholic beverages are prohibited on Navajoland.
4. Please stay on the designated self guided roads unless accompanied by a tour guide
5. Rock climbing and off-trail hiking are prohibited
6. Fires are permitted only in grills and fireplaces or in similar controlled devices. No open ground fires in campgrounds.
7. Do not disturb or remove animals, plants, rocks or artifacts.
8. Please observe quiet hours from 11:00 pm to 6:00 am at all camping areas.
9. The use of firearms is prohibited on the Navajo Nation.
10. The Navajo Nation is not responsible for any injuries, accidents, or thefts of personal property while traveling through the reservation.
11. Please restrict travel to designated trails and established routes. Off-road travel by four-wheel vehicles, dune buggies, jeeps and motorcycles is prohibited on back country roads.
12. Photography for personal use is allowed. However, permission to photograph the Navajo residents and their property is required. A gratuity is expected. Photography for commercial use requires a permit.

Discover Navajoland, Visitor's Guide

2. to litter to leave things around a place so as to make it untidy **trash** rubbish **refuse** ['refjuːs] **3. beverage** ['bevərɪdʒ] something to drink **to prohibit** [prəˈhɪbɪt] to forbid **4. to designate** to mark **to accompany** to go with sb **5. off-trail** away from the marked path **6. to permit** [-'--] to allow **device** thing made for a special purpose **7. to disturb** to break up the quiet of sb or sth **to remove** to take away **9. firearm** gun **10. theft** *Diebstahl* **property** thing or things owned **traveling** (Brit travelling) **11. to restrict** to limit **established route** *ausgewiesene Strecke* **12. permission** [-'--] act of allowing sb to do sth **resident** inhabitant **to require** to need **gratuity** *Trinkgeld* **commercial** (adj) intended to make a profit **permit** ['--] official written licence

68 The Southwest

User Permits, Licences & Fees

Permits for Hiking, Camping and Backcountry Use:
Navajo Parks & Recreation Department
P.O. Box 9000
Window Rock, AZ 86515
(520) 871-6636 or 6647
Fax (520)871-6637 or 7040

Licence for Hunting, Fishing, Trapping and Boating:
Navajo Fish & Wildlife
P.O. Box 1480
Window Rock, AZ 86515
(520) 871-6451 or 6452
Fax (520)871-7040

Permits for Commercial Photography:
Office of Broadcast Services
P.O. Box 2310
Window Rock, AZ 86515
(520) 871-6655 or 6656
Fax (520) 871-7355

Reservation time

Arizona time

What Time Is It??

The Navajo Reservation, although mostly in Arizona, observes Daylight Savings Time from April 6 to October 26. This is the same time as New Mexico. The rest of Arizona and the Hopi Reservation remain on Mountain Standard Time.

Role Play

Read and follow the instructions.

Setting: at one of the Navajo Nation parks

Preparation
Form groups of 4 to 5 people.
Roles: One group acts as Navajo park rangers. The members of the other groups act as German tourists touring the Southwest.

Tasks
Study the given information about the park rules and regulations, about permits, licences and fees, and about the time.

Navajo park rangers
Prepare statements to explain the rules and regulations to the tourists.

German tourists
Prepare questions you would like to ask.

Form new groups which include one park ranger and several tourists. You have just arrived at one of the Navajo Nation parks and have some questions for the park ranger.

Window Rock, the landmark of the namesake capital of the Navajo reservation

Home To Many Cultures

Going beyond the text If you would like more information, you may contact the Navajo Nation, P.O. Box 308, Window Rock, AZ 89515.
(Internet → http://www.heritage.tnc.org./nhp/us/navajo/)

Without Title

for my Father who lived without ceremony

It's hard you know without the buffalo,
the shaman, the arrow,
but my father went out each day to hunt
as though he had them.
5 He worked in the stockyards.
All his life he brought us meat.
No one marked his first kill,
no one sang his buffalo song.
Without a vision he had migrated to the city
10 and went to work in the packing house.
When he brought home his horns and hides
my mother said
get rid of them.
I remember the animal tracks of his car
15 out the drive in snow and mud,
the aerial on his old car waving
like a bow string.
I remember the silence of his lost power,
the red buffalo painted on his chest.
20 Oh, I couldn't see it
but it was there, and in the night I heard
his buffalo grunts like a snore.

Diane Glancy

Understanding the poem
1. Who is the speaker?
2. Explain in your own words what the speaker points out about her father's life.

Analysing the poem
Find the poetic elements and analyse how the poet uses them to describe her childhood memories.

---

2 shaman [´ʃɑːmən] priest and medicine man **5 stockyard** large enclosure for cattle awaiting slaughter **9 to migrate** to move to **11 hide** skin of an animal **16 aerial** [´eəriəl] antenna **17 bow** [bəʊ] *Bogen* **string** a thin cord **22 grunt** *Grunzen*

Discussing the poem

1. What was the speaker's relationship to her father like?
2. What idea of the American Indians' experience does the poem convey? Compare your findings with what you have learned about the Navajos.

Creative writing

Create a title based on the poem's subject.

Pre-reading activity

Study the pictures and the chart. What information do you get and what impressions do these pictures convey?

The Mexican-American Border: A Golden Door?

Cooperating cops: US border patrol inspector and Mexican police officers meet on the El Paso side of the Rio Grande. Greater cooperation between both countries' police may have aided El Paso's steady drop in crime.

cop (infml) police officer

Home To Many Cultures

Crackdown shifts the problem

Every time the U.S. Border Patrol has stepped up enforcement efforts in one sector of the border, illegal immigrants have sought other points of entry. Operation Gatekeeper, begun in San Diego in 1994, has reduced immigration and other illegal activity there. But the trouble simply shifted east – to the El Centro, Calif., and McAllen, Texas, sectors.

Illegal Mexican immigrants leap from the border fence into the United States along the U.S.-Mexico border.

Hot On The Trail

Along the 2000-mile-long Mexican-American border there is a lot of business going on in each direction. Mexicans living along the border shop at the supermarkets on the American side since some groceries are cheaper there. On the other hand, the Americans go for day trips to Mexico to enjoy Mexican life and food. The official border crossings along the US-Mexican border can be passed by US and Mexicans citizens in each direction provided they possess proper documents. Nevertheless, there is massive illegal immigration from Mexico into the US. Many of the illegal immigrants stay in the border regions of the Southwest as undocumented workers.

DULZURA, Calif. Elias Herrera reins his big horse to a halt, turns in the saddle, creaking leather, looks down and counts. "Five, six, seven." He is pointing at tracks left along a fire-scarred ridge in the Otay Mountains east of San Diego. It is very dry, and the twilight air smells like hot grass and warm horses. He rides on, reading the signs, how worn or fresh, how deep or sharp, what the dew or wind has done.
Elias Herrera is tracking humans.
He is good at this, and lists the brand names of the shoes and sneakers that left the signs. He has tracked high heels through the desert, and bare feet. This evening, based on the size of the prints, he guesses five men, plus a woman and

---

crackdown severe measures to restrict or discourage undesirable or criminal people or actions **to shift** to change the direction or focus of sth **to step up** to increase the amount, speed or intensity of sth **enforcement** the action of making sure that a law, rule, etc is obeyed **to seek** (pt, pp sought) to look for, to try to find **to decline** to decrease **apprehension** the action of arresting sb, esp by the police **to soar** to rise quickly to a high level

1 to rein [reɪn] to pull a horse to a stop **2 to creak** to make a harsh sound **4/5 fire-scarred** destroyed by a fire **5 ridge** Bergkamm **9 dew** Tau

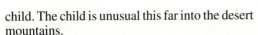 The Southwest

child. The child is unusual this far into the desert mountains.

"They came across this morning," Herrera says, and they were moving north, of course, from Mexico, from the border, which out here is not marked by fence or river, but is real enough, just five miles away.

It could have taken the group two days to reach this spot, hiding by day, darting forward at night, trying to elude not only the horses but everything else.

Where are they now?

Herrera squints, shrugs. "Could be laid up waiting for dark somewhere," he says. "Could be in L.A."

Herrera is a leader of the U.S. Border Patrol's Mounted Unit, San Diego sector, and under his command are about 20 agents who ride the mountains and canyons far east of the city, in terrain too rough and isolated for trucks. They do this at night, some nights so dark a rider can't see farther than a horse's ears, can't see the barbed wire until he feels it, can't see the ravines that fall off like the sides of buildings.

While the debate over the costs and benefits of illegal immigration continues in the state capitals and Washington, out here in these beautifully rough badlands, things are reduced to the elements. Heat and rock. Smugglers and crossers – the *polleros* and *pollos*. And, of course, *la migra,* the border patrol. […]

Herrera looks around him. He is a big solid man. His father's family still has relatives back in Mexico, but he has no regrets, he says, about his job. "This is respectable work," he says.

William Booth

The Washington Post National Weekly Edition, September 1, 1997

Understanding the text
1. Describe Elias Herrera's job.
2. How does he track down illegal immigrants?

Discussing the text
What does Elias Herrera mean by "This is respectable work"?

Creative writing
Write a story about an escape using these words: barbed wire, dart, elude, ravine, ridge, rough, trail, tracks.

---

24 to dart to move quickly **25 to elude** to escape **28 to squint** to look at sb/sth with eyes partly shut in order to see better **to shrug** to raise one's shoulders **to lay up** to hide **31 patrol** [pəˈtrəʊl] **32 mounted** here: on horseback **37/38 barbed wire** *Stacheldraht* **38 ravine** [rəˈviːn] canyon **43 badlands** desert-like territory **45 pollero** (Mex sl) *Schlepper* **pollo** (Mex sl) illegal immigrant **46 la migra** (Mex infml) US Border Patrol **47 solid** strong and muscular

Home To Many Cultures

Along The Rio Grande

The lower Rio Grande was for long no more than a farming area (though a fertile one, with a growing season of 340 days). Its population has soared over the past 20 years to today's 1.2m. It could well double again by 2005.

Moreover, no matter how fast the American border economies grow, officially recorded unemployment remains high – at 8-16%, from one area to another – so great is the pool of unemployed labour waiting on the Mexican side of the frontier. Yet if there is any ill feeling towards immigrants, local Americans will tell you time and again, it is stirred up by outsiders.

That is less of a tribute to the *norte-americanos* than it sounds. Most American communities near the border are by now predominantly Latino, their leaders usually second- or third-generation Mexican-Americans. And whereas their civic competence is typically American, other aspects of border life are not. Ultra-formal coming-out parties are held for 15-year-old girls, who are known, along with the occasions, as *quinceaneras*. The border language is an appealing one that swings from Spanish into English and back again in a single sentence. For instance, at a coming-out party: "That chico es muy simpatico, pero su acne is a real turn-off."

It is not just cultural ties that bind the American border communities to Mexico. The *maquiladora* programme has revitalised the region, notably in south Texas. For every plant on the Mexican side, there is usually at least a warehousing operation on the American side. If a *maquiladora's* managers are American, they commute across the border each day. Moreover, Mexicans love to spend their money on American goods, which, for them at least, spell high quality. […] Average income per head on the American side is at least twice, and in some areas as much as six times, the average income across the border. Hence the growing number of Mexicans filling the American side.

The Economist, December 12, 1992

San Antonio
Facts

San Antonio occupies an area of 388.6 square miles in south central Texas, about 140 miles north of the Gulf of Mexico.

Racial/Ethnic distribution
City of San Antonio: (1990)
Spanish Lang./Surname 55.6%
Anglo 35.9%
Black 7.0%
Other Races 1.5%
Source: U.S. Bureau of Census-1990

Population:
City of San Antonio 1,114,800

Source: Planning Department, City of San Antonio

---

4 to soar to rise quickly to a high level **13 to stir up** here: to start, to cause **16 predominant** most noticeable **19 civic competence** here: abilitiy to cope with life in a city **21 coming-out party** party given for a girl's first official appearance in society **24 appealing** (adj) attractive **28 tie** connection **30 maquiladora** (Mex) foreign-owned factory in Mexico at which imported parts are assembled by lower-paid workers into products for export **to revitalise** [riːˈvaɪtəlaɪz] to put new life into **31 notably** especially **plant** factory **41 hence** for this reason

Internet   Hispanic-Americans → http://www.hisp.com

Internet   San Antonio → http://www.ci.sat.tx.us

Understanding the text	What do you learn about the economic, social and cultural life in the border communities?
Discussing the text	Study the facts about San Antonio and compare your findings with what you have learned about the economic, social and cultural life in the border communities. Prepare a short oral statement.

So Long 'Dallas,' Hello High Tech

As computers become more important than oil, Texas offers new promise and dangers.

At 26, John Carmack faces a problem that confronts few GenXers: what should he do with his extra Ferrari? From his office in the Dallas suburbs, Carmack has made a fortune in computer games. His company, id Software, cranks out the hottest titles in the business – each with ominous names like Quake and Doom, one of the most popular cybergames ever. It's a Texas success story: Carmack came here in 1992, attracted by the low taxes, warm weather and thriving computer industry. With just a dozen employees, he clears more than $20 million. The profits enable Carmack to fulfill his Italian-roadster fantasies – and then some. "Four Ferraris I don't need," he says.

Carmack is a model of today's rich Texan, a breed that now makes its millions in computers, not crude oil. Just over 10 years ago, the oil-price collapse pummeled the state. But the crash opened the way to a new economy. High-tech firms took advantage of cheap labor and foreclosed land. By luck as much as design, Texas employment growth led the nation from 1990 to 1996. It has now passed New York as the second most populous state. The trend is gathering speed: Texas is growing faster than California, and it attracts more tourists than Florida. More than a quarter Hispanic, Texas is America – circa 2050. […]

The idea of the state as leading indicator is not without its downside: it has more parolees than any state and the country's worst water pollution. Meanwhile, Texans pride themselves on their unique culture – McDonald's and Miller Lite even conduct Texas-specific ad campaigns, filled with twangy accents and Texas maps. But now the Lone Star isn't just rising by itself: it's pulling the country.

Newsweek, April 21, 1997

---

3 GenXer member of "Generation X", those people born in the late 1950s, 1960s and early 1970s **6 fortune** large amount of money **6/7 id Software** name of company which makes computer software **7 to crank out** here: to produce **8 ominous** [ˈɒmɪnəs] **12 thriving** prospering **13 to clear** here: to earn as a profit **20 to pummel** to hit, to beat **23 to foreclose** to take possession of sb's property, usu because they have not paid pack an agreed part of a loan **31 indicator** *Messlatte* **32 parolee** [pəˈrəʊliː] person who was released from prison before the end of his/her sentence **35/36 Miller Lite** brand of beer **37 twangy accent** *näselnder Akzent;* Southern twang, accent typical of the South **38 Lone Star** nickname of the State of Texas, which has a single star on its flag. This single star recalls the time when Texas was an independent republic (1836–1845) before it joined the US.

Home To Many Cultures

Understanding the text
1. Explain the title.
2. John Carmack embodies today's Texas. What is it like?
3. What was Texas' traditional source of wealth?
4. The Lone Star state has always considered itself something special. How does this still show?

Discussing the text
Could John Carmack's success and career be a role model for you? Comment on this question.

Translate
Lines 31–39.

Working with thematic vocabulary
Assume you have to write a report about the Southwest. To prepare your report make a list of terms and words you will need to give a comprehensive description. Group them in thematic categories.

Great Britain: Regional Perspectives

Top left: The Queen reviews her Tower of London guards – the Beefeaters. Top right: The pub is an important part of social life in the U.K., as it is where people go to meet others. Middle: The Welsh dragon as it appears on Wales' flag. Above: Cricket is a popular summer sport in the U.K. Left: The British always talk about the weather. They are still talking about the great storm of 1988.

Regional Perspectives

Getting to know the British

Look at the statistics below. Which pieces of information do you find most surprising and why?

Unemployment … has fallen to 1.5 million, the lowest level for 17 years.

Television … is watched 25 hours a week by U.K. citizens, who spend an average of £ 12 per person per year on videos.

Life expectancy … in Britain is over 74 years for men and 79 for women.

A job for life … is a thing of the past, says 82% of the population.

Fish and chips … is still the nation's most favoured fast food: 47% of the population ranks it number one. But Britain also has 8,000 curry houses.

21 million cars … travel on British roads today, compared to only 3.7 million 40 years ago. 30.1 million Britons are licensed to drive.

31.1% of people … took more than one vacation last year; 28% chose perennial favorite Spain as their destination of choice.

45% of the population … believe in ghosts.

Churchgoers … number 6.4 million mainstream Christian believers, compared to 9.1 million in the 1970s. Another 600,000 regularly attend non-Trinitarian churches and 1.3 million worship in other religions.

British homes … are getting warmer. 67.9% of households are equipped with central heating, 18.5% have double glazing.

182 million cups of tea … are consumed each day by 77% of the population; Britain imports 20.1 million bottles of champagne – more than any other country in the world – and exports 114.5 million bottles of whisky.

27 million people read … at least one national newspaper every day; of those, 12% read broadsheet newspapers, while 56.8 % read tabloids.

Population … England has 48,903,400 inhabitants, Scotland 5,136,000 inhabitants and Wales 2,916,800 inhabitants.(Census 1997)
Mairi Ben Brahim
Time, October 27, 1997

---

to rank to place sth in a position on a scale **perennial** constantly occurring **mainstream** normal, conventional **Trinitarian** relating to the Holy Trinity **to worship** to show your respect for a god eg by praying **equipped with** supplied with **double glazing** two layers of glass fitted to a window **broadsheet** large format **tabloid** newspaper with small pages containing short articles and a lot of photographs

"Rich South, Poor North" Tell That To The Cornish

"Rich South, poor North" is still the typical cliché about Britain today. Surveys have shown that the north-south divide exists in terms of prosperity, the standard of living, social conditions and unemployment. However, there are exceptions to this overall trend.

Most Britons think of Cornwall, England's most south-westerly county, as a lovely place to spend a summer holiday, blessed by sea, sand and beautiful, rugged scenery. So it is – but then few of those visitors have trudged through Redruth on a grey, blustery day in February. In the steep main street a couple of shops are empty; four or five others have been taken over by charities: at the bottom of the hill is the shell of an old market building. Just outside the town is a more dramatic symbol of economic decline: the county's (and Europe's) last tin mine, South Crofty, due to close on March 6th with the loss of 170-odd jobs.

The main effect of South Crofty's closure is just that: symbolic. The heyday of Cornish tin mining was more than a century ago, and came only after much bigger money had been made in copper. But the death of tin neatly illustrates the source of Cornwall's economic difficulties. The best days of other traditional industries, such as china clay and fishing, are also long gone. Farming is in slump, as it is all over Britain. A lot of jobs in tourism are seasonal and poorly paid. [...]

What holds the economy back? One problem is geography. It is 200 miles from London to Cornwall's eastern border, and the county is 80 miles from east to west. Although transport links have improved in recent years, they could still be much better. Trains run more slowly from, say, London to Cornwall than to the north-east. And a few miles of the A30 trunk road are not yet dual carriageway. Sometimes lorries hit a railway bridge there, causing long traffic jams. [...]

But there is another problem. Cornwall's 480,000 people are scattered: the biggest town, St. Austell, has a mere 21,000 souls. This makes it unlikely that job problems could be solved by a few new big employers. Cornwall's prospects therefore depend on creating and attracting a lot of successful small and medium-sized companies.

The Economist, March 7, 1998

The last shift

---

4 county administrative division of Britain, the largest unit of local government **6 to be blessed by** to be fortunate in having sth **7 rugged** ['--] rough and uneven, with many rocks **10 to trudge** to walk with slow, heavy steps **11/12 blustery** with strong winds **17 charity** society or organisation for helping people in need **18 shell** structure that forms a framework **20 tin** Zinn **24 heyday** ['--] the time of great success for sth **26/27 copper** Kupfer **30 china clay** fine white clay used for the manufacture of porcelain **31 slump** period when business is bad **51 trunk road** (Brit) important main road **52 dual carriageway** (Brit) road with a central strip to separate traffic moving in different directions **58 mere** [mɪə(r)] bloß **60 employer** person or organisation that one works for **prospects** (pl) the chances of being successful

Regional Perspectives 79

Understanding the text

1. What two contrasting views of Cornwall does the author describe?
2. Why is the closure of the South Crofty tin mine symbolic for Cornwall?
3. What other factors are having a negative effect on the Cornish economy?
4. *"Rich South, Poor North" Tell That To The Cornish.* Explain this title in relation to the text.

Going beyond the text

1. Which regions of Germany have mining industries and what is the state of these industries today? How do the closures of mines or other industries affect the people in those regions?
2. "Rich South, poor North." Could Germany be described in this way? Give reasons for your answer.

Working with the language

Complete the mind map. Collect words connected with *transport* from the text. Then add any others you can think of.

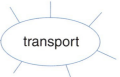

Translate

Lines 36–55.
Remember when translating you want to produce a good German text. Think about the register (fml or infml) of the text and the use of prepositions.

The Millennium Dome

London Landmarks: An artist's impression of how the Millennium Dome in Greenwich will look.

 Great Britain

The Millennium Dome, which will open in the London suburb of Greenwich on 31 December 1999, is intended to be a dramatic interpretation of the millennium. It will be the largest cable and fabric structure ever to be constructed, forming the centrepiece of a 130-acre festival site.

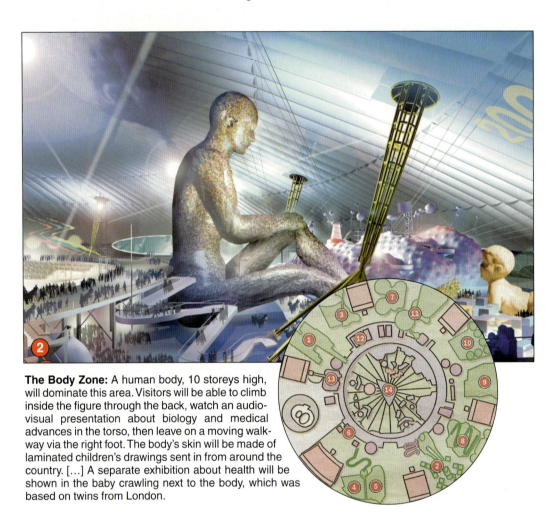

The Body Zone: A human body, 10 storeys high, will dominate this area. Visitors will be able to climb inside the figure through the back, watch an audio-visual presentation about biology and medical advances in the torso, then leave on a moving walkway via the right foot. The body's skin will be made of laminated children's drawings sent in from around the country. [...] A separate exhibition about health will be shown in the baby crawling next to the body, which was based on twins from London.

---

fabric *Stoff* **torso** main part of the human body, not including the head, arms and legs **storey** floor **laminated** [ˈlæmɪneɪtɪd] *laminiert* **to crawl** [krɔːl] to move on hands and knees

Internet Millennium Dome → http://www.mx 2000. co. uk/thedome.htm

Regional Perspectives

Visitors to the new Dome, a structure big enough to house 13 Albert Halls, would have "the most exciting day out in the world," said Tony Blair at last week's launch.
Twelve zones, each with a different theme, will fan out from a central piazza, which will be the backdrop for a sound and light performance repeated several times a day. The singer Peter Gabriel has been chosen to compose the music for this "backdrop" because of his interest in sounds from around the world. Mark Fisher, who has designed sets for Pink Floyd and U2 will be in charge of lighting and laser shows. [...]
Details of the Licensed to Skill and The Learning Curve sections were also released. They will be deliberately interwoven on two levels to show the need for people to continue learning throughout their careers.
Visitors will be able to put on virtual reality helmets to explore different jobs. There will be three "pools" of information to dip into – a paddling pool if visitors want to dabble with a particular career, a swimming pool to go deeper and a diving pool if they want to "dive into the heart" of a particular area of work.
They will be shown the "classroom of the future," linked up with schools across the country on the Internet. Children will be able to telephone a special hotline to Downing Street to tell Mr. Blair what they want to do when they grow up.

The Weekly Telegraph, March 4, 1998

Understanding the text

1. The dome will have ten zones or sections. What information will visitors be able to obtain in the 'Licensed to Skill' and 'The Learning Curve' sections?
2. What will be the main attractions of 'The Body Zone'?

Going beyond the text

How does the Millennium Dome differ from other theme parks and expositions you know?

Analysing the text

Comment on the metaphors used to describe the 'pools' of information.

---

2 Royal Albert Hall famous concert hall in London named after Prince Albert, the husband of Queen Victoria **6 to fan out** to spread from a central point **piazza** [pi'ætsə] public square **7 backdrop** background scenery **12 Pink Floyd, U2** rock bands **17 interwoven** closely linked **20/21 helmet** hard hat **22 to dip into** here: to look at sth briefly **23 paddling pool** shallow pool **to dabble** here: to study sth without serious intentions **30 Downing Street** street in London where the Prime Minister's official residence is

 Great Britain

Britain's Cities Are Booming

Britain's cities are booming thanks to a reviving economy and changed attitudes to urban living.

It wasn't supposed to happen this way. In the 1980s Britain's cities looked fated to a long slow decline as the middle class succumbed to the lure of green countryside, or a suburban pastiche of it. Telecommunications and computers were making the hard slog into work unnecessary for growing numbers. Retailers were following, as they did years ago in America, to out-of-town shopping malls.

Those left behind were mostly the rich and the poor. The future of cities looked bleak. But that is not the way things have turned out. Instead, all these trends look as if they may have gone into reverse. Rather than declining, Britain's cities are booming.

London is once again humming (or "swinging" – take your pick). Its economy is growing twice as fast as the nation's as a whole. A range of London-based industries, from finance to theatre to fashion, are booming. Elsewhere, city centres have become huge construction sites as their economies, and populations, revive. […]

From Coventry to Glasgow the shops are full; restaurants and cafes are crowded; house prices are rising and jobs are on offer.

Much of this activity is, of course, the direct result of Britain's long economic expansion. But wider trends also seem to be contributing to the urban revival. It is not just greater numbers of young people who wish to live in cities, but people of all ages, including the old. The popu-

In 1997, the *Angel of the North* was erected in the town of Gateshead in the north-east of England. Antony Gormley's statue is a 20-metre high steel sculpture. A local politician said: "This is to Gateshead what the Eiffel Tower is to Paris and The Statue of Liberty to New York."

---

to boom to increase and develop at a fast rate **urban** ['--] relating to a city **4 fated** destined **5 decline** worsening situation **6 to succumb** [sə'kʌm] to give in to **7 lure** [lʊə(r)] attractive quality **9 pastiche** [-'-] imitation **12 slog** tiring effort **14 retailer** ['---] trader **17/18 shopping mall** large covered area that contains many different shops and in which traffic is not allowed **22 bleak** gloomy, depressing **26/27 to go into reverse** here: to happen in the opposite way **44 revival** cf to revive: to become successful again

Regional Perspectives

lation of inner London has begun once again to increase.

After years of population loss, other cities are also growing once again. The appeal of the suburbs has been tarnished by growing congestion and longer travel times. [...]

City planners are keen to attract people back into city centres as places to live, as well as to work. More inner-city flats, houses and pedestrianised shopping areas are being built. Beauty, which has been low on city architects' agendas for much of the latter years of the 20th century, is now recognised to be as important as function. Britain's booming cities are not immune to the social problems common to all western cities. Too many pockets of poverty survive amid the general prosperity, and are all the more glaring because the rest of the city is thriving. Yet despite these problems, British cities are right to approach the future with confidence. The signs that point to further expansion and prosperity are impossible to ignore. Tourism, telecommunications, leisure, luxury retailing, financial and information services – which flourish as well if not better in city centres as anywhere else – are all big growth industries.

The Economist, August 2, 1997

Understanding the text

1. What was the situation in Britain's cities in the 1980s?
2. How have the cities changed in the late 1990s? Give reasons for this urban revival.
3. What negative aspect of city life is discussed?
4. How does the author see the future of British cities?

Going beyond the text

1. Discuss the advantages and disadvantages of attracting more and more people into the cities.
2. Which cities in Germany are booming? What are the reasons for this development?

Working with the language

Find the corresponding verbs and adjectives for the following nouns:
decline, economy, construction, revival, increase, loss, attraction, prosperity, retailer, information

noun	verb	adjective
decline	to decline	declining
economy	???	???
construction	???	???

Translate Lines 30–48.

---

50 appeal quality that is attractive **51 to tarnish** to damage the reputation **congestion** [kənˈdʒestʃən] the state of being too crowded **57 agenda** [əˈdʒendə] list of points for discussion **63 prosperity** wealth **64 to thrive** to flourish, to be successful

Great Britain

Business success means being in the right place at the right time.

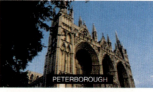

TELFORD

The cradle of the industrial revolution and now a truly modern town. A magnet for successful companies here and abroad.

MILTON KEYNES

The UK's fastest growing city, home to over 3,500 prospering businesses, with half of Britain's population within 80 minutes.

WARRINGTON

Strategically located between Manchester and Liverpool, at the focal point of the UK's biggest concentration of motorways.

PETERBOROUGH

The focus of the country's fastest growing region, this ancient cathedral city is ready to meet the needs of the future with new communication links and modern infrastructure.

PRESTON

Close to the Ribble Valley, a key town in an area of the UK with a booming economy larger than that of some European countries.

NORTHAMPTON

This major industrial and commercial centre successfully combines the best of old and new and is now one of the fastest growing areas in Britain.

In today's volatile business environment, success depends on strategic location.

Industry and commerce alike need rapid, easy access to key markets and suppliers, here and abroad. Access provided by major communication arteries: motorways, key rail routes, airports, and seaports.

CNT is England's largest owner of development land in a series of locations designed for business success. Like the six shown here, built from day one with business in mind or transformed by new communication links.

A strategic location isn't the only benefit. They all offer an enthusiastic welcome to new companies seeking growth and expansion. They have established business infrastructures. Their workforces are young, dynamic, forward-looking. They are ideal places to live, in attractive environments, with a wide range of excellent housing, shops, sports and leisure facilities.

However, looking for the right location often takes more time, trouble and money than you can easily afford.

Talk to CNT. We're ready to help you find business success in these locations.

LOCATIONS MADE FOR BUSINESS SUCCESS.

CNT SELLS LAND FOR THE DEVELOPMENT OF BUSINESS PREMISES IN KEY LOCATIONS THROUGHOUT ENGLAND.
ASK ABOUT: ♦ DEVELOPMENT SITES. ♦ FAST-TRACK PLANNING. ♦ CONFIDENTIAL AND COMPREHENSIVE SERVICE.

---

volatile ['vɒlətaɪl] unstable, changing suddenly **business environment** business world **location** place, site **access** ['ækses] entry **supplier** [-'--] sb who provides you with sth **abroad** in a foreign country **CNT** Commission for the New Towns **to transform** to change completely **benefit** advantage **infrastructure** [--'--] basic structures and facilities **workforce** the people who work for a company etc **premises** (pl) ['premɪsɪz] land and buildings **fast-track planning** quick or rapid planning **comprehensive** [,--'--] that includes everything

cradle birthplace **prospering** (adj) ['---] rich and successful **focal point** centre of activity **ancient** ['eɪnʃənt] very old

Internet   CNT → http://www.cnt.org.uk

Regional Perspectives

Understanding the text

1. What service does CNT offer?
2. Explain the term 'strategic location.'
3. What other factors are important for the success of a location?
4. Explain why the six centres shown in the photos are strategic business locations.

Woking with the language

Go through the text and find words and phrases that describe an ideal business location. Arrange them in an order of importance.

Going beyond the text

Work in groups. Imagine you are going to start up in business. Firstly, decide what kind of business it will be. Then write a description of the ideal location for your business, giving reasons for your choice.

Working with thematic vocabulary

Collect the thematic vocabulary from the texts you have read so far and list the words under the headings:

city   **business**

Prepare a short presentation on one of these topics:
Life in the City Today or Business Today

Pre-reading activity

What do you associate with Scotland?

Scotland's Cultural Cocktail

Tourism is an important source of income for many regions of Scotland. Visitors can get an insight into the history and cultural traditions by participating in the wide variety of events and festivals which take place around Scotland throughout the year.

If you think Scotland amounts to a quaint collage of haggis, tartan and misty days, think again. [...]
Scotland's beautiful hills and glens are only part of the story. The rest is a dynamic cultural cocktail of everything from Highland games to

---

1 quaint [kweɪnt] curious and old-fashioned **1/2 collage** ['kɒlɑːʒ] collection of unrelated things **2 haggis** ['hægɪs] Scottish dish made from sheep's heart, lungs and liver and boiled in a bag made from part of a sheep's stomach **tartan** ['--] woollen cloth with a check pattern **misty** cf mist, thick cloud, fog **4 glen** narrow valley

world-class arts festivals; informal folk gatherings in local pubs to Scottish Opera performances. […]

Sporting days are promised in the nation's Highland games. Contrary to popular belief, you don't have to be in the wilds of Scotland to enjoy this peculiar mix of athletics: Highland dancing, piping, carnival entertainments and tug-of-wars. Taking place in parks and fields all over Scotland from Aberdeen to St. Andrews and the Isle of Skye to Dunoon, the games are an ideal chance for families to forget their inhibitions and toss the caber. […]

For far-flung festivities, Shetland offers its own brand of culture. The island's capital town of Lerwick is lit up each January with the spectacular ritual burning of a Viking longship. Up-Helly-Aa is a fascinating step into another age and an opportunity for visitors to immerse themselves in Shetland's historical links with Scandinavia.

The Sword Dance

The Skye Folk Festival each July offers visitors a chance to sample the northwestern island's culture at its finest. Based in Portree, the festival features concerts by local and international bands, traditional Scottish dances (ceilidhs) and workshops. […]

An obvious pitstop for culture vultures is Edinburgh – each August the city hosts an orgy of arts as the world comes to

Tossing the caber

---

18 peculiar strange, unusual **20 piping** ['paɪpɪŋ] playing the bagpipes **21/22 tug-of-war** sport in which two teams test their strength by pulling on opposite ends of a rope **28 inhibition** [,--'--] feeling of worry and fear **tossing the caber** ['keɪbə(r)] sport in which a tree trunk is thrown **29 far-flung** distant **30 brand** type, sort **34 to immerse in sth** to involve oneself deeply in sth, to absorb oneself in sth **40 to sample** to try sth by experiencing it **47 ceilidh** ['keɪli] **49 pitstop** here: short visit **50 culture vulture** (infml) person who loves culture **52 to host** to organise an event to which others are invited **52 orgy** (infml) ['ɔːdʒi] here: great variety

Regional Perspectives

visit the International Festival and Fringe, the Military Tattoo, Film Festival and Jazz Festival. But Scotland's arts scene is burgeoning from Plockton to Paisley. […]

Scotland's events calendar brims with traditional celebrations, beginning with Hogmanay. A unique welcome to the New Year, it throws complete strangers into one another's arms. At midnight, the bells are heralded at home or by large crowds gathered in public places, before the ritual of first footing friends' and families' homes begins.

For a spectacular salute, Edinburgh hosts a three-day celebration leading up to New Year, involving family entertainment, traditional dances, classical music concerts and fun fairs. It culminates in a Hogmanay spectacular in the city centre, with live music, fireworks and pipe bands. […]

Burns Night on 25 January is a tribute to Scotland's national poet, Robert Burns. The traditional Burns supper, complete with the legendary haggis, neeps (turnips) and tatties (potatoes), is a dewey-eyed celebration of all things Scottish – one open to all, irrespective of nationality. […]

Kathleen Morgan

Scottish Tourist Board, 1995

Haggis

Discussing the text — Which of the events described in the brochure would you like to visit? Say why they appeal to you.

Going beyond the text — Compare New Year traditions in Germany to Hogmanay traditions in Scotland.

Working with the language — Collect all the adjectives from the text which give a positive impression about Scotland. For example: (line 4) *beautiful*.

Creative writing — A group of students from a school abroad is going to visit your town. Write an article describing cultural events and festivals in your region that you think would be of interest.

---

55 fringe events which take part during a festival but are not an official part of it **Military Tattoo** [tə'tuː] public display of military marching, exercises and music **57 to burgeon** ['bɜːdʒən] to grow quickly **59 to brim with** to be or become full of sth **61 Hogmanay** (Scot) ['hɒgməneɪ] New Year in Scotland **64 to herald** to greet with enthusiasm **66/67 first footing** cf first foot: the first person to enter a house at Hogmanay **79 turnip** *Rübe* **80 dewey-eyed** [ˌ--'-] starry-eyed, emotional **81 irrespective of** not taking account of or considering sth/sb

Internet Scotland → http://www.scotland.rampant.com/

 Great Britain

Pre-reading activity: Look at the photo. Describe the school and its location and compare it to your own school.

A Vision Of The Highlands

Even in the remotest corners of Scotland, the latest technological developments are becoming a part of everyday life.

Ulva Ferry Primary School, Mull.

One thing made it difficult for the children of Argyll to learn their Physics, French and History.

Geography.

The Western Highlands. Beautiful. Windswept. And remote.

80% of the schools here have fewer than three teachers.

It's not unusual to find children of twelve sitting in the same class as five year olds.

The local education authority asked if BT could help. Our solution was something called Campus Vision.

It's based on the videoconferencing technology widely used in the business world, where high quality images and sound are sent along digital phone lines.

Except that now it enables children in remote villages to join other schools for lessons. (It's ironic. While everyone else is doing their best to reduce class sizes, we're increasing them.)

So now twelve year olds can study physics with their contemporaries, while younger pupils can tackle the three 'r's with children the same age. (Campus Vision is so straightforward even a five year old can use it.)

It's not just the pupils who benefit either. Teachers can take part in staff meetings and training courses without spending time and money travelling.

Campus Vision is just one of the ways in which BT helps students and teachers. There's Campus World, an area on the Internet specially designed to be used during lessons.

And Home Campus, an on-line home learning service. (Instead of getting Dad to help with the homework, children can ask their computer.)

BT helps people from all walks of life. If you'd like to know more, call us on Free*fone 0800* 800 848 or find us on www.bt.com.

---

windswept exposed to strong winds **remote** isolated **local education authority** local government having the power to make decisions about school matters **BT** British Telecom **to enable sb to do sth** to make it possible for sb to do sth **contemporary** [-'---] person of about the same age **the three 'r's** reading, writing and arithmetic **staff** (pl) here: the teachers in a school **walk of life** profession, occupation or position in society

Understanding the text

1. What are the advantages of Campus Vision for both pupils and teachers in the Western Highlands of Scotland?
2. Describe the other services available to help students and teachers.

Going beyond the text

1. Do you think services like those offered by BT will become available everywhere in the future?
2. How do you foresee the 'schools of the future' in your country?

Pride Of Lions

Geddes Thomson

Glasgow, the largest city in Scotland, has a large number of immigrants from India and Pakistan. In this short story, the Scottish writer Geddes Thomson looks at the racial problems facing an immigrant in Glasgow.

I was twenty-one. I had just left university after completing a degree in English. I knew nothing. I wanted to be a writer. I was working on the Glasgow buses as a conductor, to see life. Later, I intended to work on the night-shift at a power station like William Faulkner and write my first novel. That would take about six weeks.

But at the moment I was sitting on the back seat of a doubledecker bus smoking a Sobranie Straight Cut cigarette. Opposite me sat my regular driver, Sardar. He was reading the Manchester *Guardian*. Not for the first time, I thought we were a strange pair to be in charge of a Glasgow bus.

I liked these day-time rests at the terminus. Passengers were few. The city had a peaceful semi-deserted look in the sunlight. The inhabitants seemed to consist of old people, young mothers and infants. Later it would be very different, as successive waves of truculent humanity invaded the bus at their appointed hours.

'Has he died yet, Sardar?' I asked.
The paper shook like a white flag in a breeze and then collapsed to show Sardar looking at me. He was never quite sure how to take my interest and always began by studying my face carefully for signs of mockery.

'He is my man,' he said. 'He fights for freedom.'
'Is he related to you, Sardar?' I knew that he wasn't, but the question would lead to further conversation.

'Sardar Singh. My name and his name. But we are not related. All Sikhs are called Singh. Did you know that?'
'Yes.'
He studied my face. 'Do you know what it means?'
'It means "lion."'
'Ah, but "Sardar"?'
'No.'
'It means "chief." I am "Chief Lion,"' he said with emphasis.
'"Sardar" is a common name. There must be a great many "Chief Lions."'
He laughed. 'Yes, a great many. Thousands and thousands.' He flung back his turbaned head and laughed. We both laughed heartily, falling back on our seats, our chests heaving with the

---

pride [praɪd] feeling of pleasure or satisfaction from doing sth well; group of lions **4 conductor** sb who sells tickets on a bus **15 terminus** last bus station at the end of the line **20 successive** one after another **truculent** (derog) [ˈtrʌkjələnt] bad-tempered and aggressive **21 appointed hours** fixed times **24 to collapse** [-ˈ-] to fall down **27 mockery** scornful, unkind action

humour of those thousands of important kings of the jungle.

'You know something, "Chief Lion"?' I said. 'It's time you were driving this bus.'

I liked him a lot. He didn't support Celtic or Rangers. He read the Manchester *Guardian* and he worried with pride about his namesake who was fasting till death in far-off India.

'Will you come for a drink with me, tonight?' he asked, picking up the hat he never wore. We arranged the place and the time.

'No overtime, tonight, then?' I asked Sardar when I met him in the pub.

He smiled. Once I had asked him how he was able to endure the long hours of queuing for overtime. He had said, 'At home I once queued for two days with my son to see the doctor. This is easy.'

After five rapid drinks Sardar was ready to come to the point.

'I have a favour to ask.'

'Fire away,' I said like a benevolent sport in one of the thrillers I despised but read in dozens.

'Could you go there and ask for the keys?' He handed me a newspaper clipping advertising a house for sale. At the bottom was the estate agent's address. 'Say you are interested in the house and wish to view it.'

I felt a flush warm my face.

'You mean -'

'They won't give me the keys. You know why.'

In his eyes I could see shame. Shame for me, for himself. A shame so palpable that it seemed to radiate out to include the people in the pub, the people in the streets beyond. I also saw fear and suppressed rage.

'Of course I'll get them.'

The next day I got the keys and we looked at the house. Sardar was pleased with it and with me. He invited me up to his flat for a meal.

'This is my friend,' he said, standing at the kitchen door.

Faces stared at me. Half-a-dozen faces which broke into smiles. The room seemed full of light. A tangy redolence tantalised my nostrils.

'Now I am in the lions' den,' I said.

Sardar laughed. He explained the joke to the others and we all laughed again.

The meal was good. We ate it with fellowship in the kitchen of that Glasgow tenement. When I left, the streets were grey and wet with rain.

Last run of our shift. A late-night bus-load of drunken and aggressive Glaswegians, who shouted, sang, swore, urinated, vomited, as the mood took them. Collecting fares required devious diplomatic gifts.

At the terminus a group of youths surrounded Sardar's cab. They chanted insults, hammered the windows with clenched fists, challenged him to come out and fight.

A pale youth with jagged blonde hair stood on the platform grinning at me.

'You just stay where you are sonny,' he said. 'You're goin nowhere.'

He couldn't have been more than fourteen. He was thin and undernourished. I was more afraid of him than I have ever been of anyone in my life.

'You like darkies?' he asked.

I couldn't answer.

'Ah asked you a question, cunty.'

I heard my voice hoarse and choked: 'They're all right. In their own country. Not over here.'

He gestured. 'C'mon.'

We walked round to the front of the bus. I could see Sardar sitting in the cab, his turban white in the gloom. He stared ahead, impassive as Buddha, as if waiting for overtime or the doctor.

53/54 Celtic, Rangers main football clubs in Glasgow **55 namesake** someone who has the same name as you **63 to endure** to face a situation patiently **to queue** [kju:] to wait in a line **70 benevolent** [bə'nevələnt] kind, helpful **71 to despise** [-'-] to dislike **74/75 estate agent** sb who sells houses and land **77 flush** blush, a flow of blood to the face that causes a red colouring **80 shame** feeling of humiliation, disgrace **81 palpable** ['pælpəbl] obvious, evident **82 to radiate** to show a strong feeling **84 to suppress** here: to control **93 tangy redolence** ['tæŋi] sharp smell **to tantalise** to excite **nostril** one of the two openings at the end of the nose, which you breathe through **94 den** the home of a wild animal **98 tenement** ['tenəmənt] building divided into flats especially in poor areas **101 Glaswegian** [glæz'wi:dʒən] inhabitant of Glasgow **103/104 devious** ['---] dishonest, sly **106 insult** hurtful expression **114 undernourished** underfed and weak **117 darkie** (offensive) dark-skinned person **119 cunty** (sl derog) an unpleasant person **120 hoarse** unclear, rough **choked** (adj) upset, angry

Regional Perspectives

'See, who ah've goat,' the youth said to his mates. 'Says he doesny like darkies in this country.'
130 'He'll have tae prove it,' a low voice said.
They crowded round and suddenly my moneybag was knocked up. A shower of coins flashed in the air.
'Better than a weddin,' one shouted as he scram-
135 bled for his share.
I heard the low voice again – 'He'll have tae prove it.'
'He'll have tae dae somethin,' the blonde youth said.
140 'Spit at him,' a voice suggested.
'Aye, that's it. Spit at the darkie.'
'C'mon, ya mug. Spit at him!'

My throat was parched with fear. I tried to swallow but couldn't. My tongue desperately searched my mouth for moisture. 145
'C'mon, spit. Spit at the darkie.'
My mouth opened. I tried to gather some saliva. My lips moved, but nothing came.
'Christ, he's no spittin. He's blowin him kisses, the pouf!' 150
I was knocked over. My body shook as the kicks thudded in. Then the sound of running feet. And silence.
Gentle hands uncurled me. Sardar's face above me. I saw with shame his concern and his pride. 155
'You are truly a lion,' he said. 'You wouldn't spit.'

Understanding the text
Identify the four scenes of the story. Then summarise each scene in two or three sentences.

Analysing the text
1. Analyse the relationship between Sardar and the narrator at the beginning of the story and describe how it changes.
2. Comment on the behaviour of the group of Glaswegian youths in the last part of the story.
3. Explain the title "Pride of Lions." Identify and discuss other references to it in the story.

Going beyond the text
Imagine you were in the same situation as the narrator. Describe how you would have reacted to the youths' attack.

Creative writing
Imagine you are a reporter for a Glasgow newspaper. Write an article about the attack described in the text.

140 to spit *spucken* **142 mug** (infml) here: stupid person **143 parched** dry **147 saliva** [sə'laɪvə] moisture in the mouth **150 pouf** [puːf] (sl derog) here: a male homosexual

Great Britain

Pre-reading activity — When do you think the photo was taken? Explain your reasons.

Hometown

"My father believed that he was bound for America, where he had a brother waiting for him. He had been in Cardiff for a couple of weeks before someone pointed out to him that he wasn't actually in New York."

For all that, Bernice Rubens is glad to claim it as her hometown. Pragmatically, her experience has served her well as a writer. "You've only got to stand on a Welsh beach to hear the musical dialogue spoken like a song."

But more than that, Rubens insists that there can have been few places better able to accommodate the dual identity of an immigrant family than the place in which she happened to have been born. "I knew I was not kosher Welsh, but inasmuch as I was unsure of my allegiances, so was the city itself. Being near the border with England gave Cardiff a rather ambiguous character. Few people spoke Welsh and those who did were considered eccentric. Part of south Wales has always hankered after the English rose and the price it paid was being viewed with suspicion by the Welsh of the north. It was neither one thing nor another, so we fitted in nicely." […]

Money was tight but lodgers helped, as did the goodwill of the Rhondda Valley miners on whom her father, Eli, relied for his living. […]

"My father would buy a couple of shirts or a pair of shoes and take his wares by bus and on foot to the valleys, where he would sell them to the miners for a shilling a week. I went with him once and I saw for myself how very deeply he was loved by those families. They were chapel-going folk and my father was a religious Jew – maybe that was part of their close understanding. He was so soft-hearted that he would waive the last payments towards the end because the stuff was usually worn out by then."

A street corner in Cardiff

---

1 bound for travelling towards **7 to claim sth** to take sth you have a right to **8/9 pragmatically** realistically **25 kosher** genuine, true **26 inasmuch as** to the extent that **27 allegiance** [əˈliːdʒəns] support, loyalty **29 ambiguous** [æmˈbɪɡjuəs] unclear, uncertain **31 eccentric** [ɪkˈsentrɪk] strange, unconventional **32 to hanker after** to have a great desire for **36 lodger** person who pays to live in sb's house **37 Rhondda Valley** coal mining area of Wales **miner** person who works underground in mines to obtain coal etc **38 to rely on** [-ˈ-] to depend on **40 wares** (pl) articles offered for sale especially in the street **47 to waive** (fml) [weɪv] not to enforce **49 stuff** (infml) things, items

⁵⁰ Post-war prosperity brought a car, a fridge, a telephone and a new house in the middle-class suburb of Penylan and saw Bernice graduate from Cardiff High School to the University of Wales. But while she confesses to being "pretty ⁵⁵ embedded in the Welsh ethos" – to the extent that almost 50 years on, the Welsh accent still returns without effort – Cardiff lacked the power to hold her. By 18, Rubens could not wait to leave.
⁶⁰ "It was a place to leave, especially if you had any artistic ambitions, which I didn't at that stage, not knowingly. People used to joke, rather unfairly, that the best thing about Cardiff was the 9.15 am to Paddington." Yet although she has lived in London ever since, her links are still ⁶⁵ strong and a deep love for Cardiff remains. "Kindness. I remember nothing but kindness and my father always acknowledged it. […] The people were deeply hospitable and Cardiff was good to us. I will always love it for the ⁷⁰ warmth with which it took us in."

Judy Goodkin

The Times Magazine, August 23, 1997

Understanding the text

1. Why does Bernice Rubens think of Cardiff as her hometown?
2. Compare Bernice Rubens' life in Cardiff before the war with post-war life.

Going beyond the text

Discuss how you would feel about leaving your hometown.

Working with the language

Look at this expression:
We're home and dry.
It means we're safe or we've been successful.

What do the following expressions mean?

An Englishman's home is his castle.
Charity begins at home.
Wherever you go there's no place like home.
That film is nothing to write home about.
Home is where the heart is.
The guests ate us out of house and home.
We get on like a house on fire.
These new bookshelves are as safe as houses.

---

50 prosperity wealth **54 to confess** to admit **55 embedded** fixed deeply **ethos** (fml) ['iːθɒs] ideas and attitudes **64 Paddington** railway station in London **65 links** connections, ties **69 hospitable** [-'---] pleased to welcome and entertain guests

Devolution In Great Britain

Devolution? That's A Pop Group, Isn't It?

Scotland and Wales have been governed by a central government from Westminster for centuries. However, after years of debate and protest in Scotland and Wales, the demands for more regional power have proved successful. Decision-making is being decentralised. This transfer of power from central government to regional parliaments or assemblies is known as devolution.

In the UK, devolution first took place in Northern Ireland in 1921, with the establishment of a parliament in Belfast. Following the outbreak of violence in Northern Ireland in 1969, the UK Government reintroduced direct rule from London.

Scotland   Wales

Milestones of Devolution

1536	Act of Union. England and Wales united. Welsh representation in English Parliament. English law and administration imposed on Wales. English became official language in Wales.
1707	Act of Union. England and Scotland united as Great Britain. Scotland represented in Parliament of Great Britain. Scots retained their own legal system, educational system and church.
1925	Plaid Cymru, Welsh nationalist party founded.
1928	Scottish Nationalist Party (SNP) founded.
1979	Devolution Referendum in Scotland. Majority vote in favour, but fell short of 40% of electorate needed to win.
1979	Devolution Referendum in Wales. Absolute majority vote against devolution.
Sept. 11, 1997	Devolution Referendum in Scotland. Majority vote for a Scottish Parliament with tax powers.
Sept. 18, 1997	Devolution Referendum in Wales. Small majority vote for a Parliamentary Assembly.
May 1999	Election of a Welsh Assembly.
May 1999	Election of a Scottish Parliament.

---

outbreak sudden start of sth **violence** behaviour which is intended to hurt or kill sb **reintroduce** to bring sth into operation again **law** [lɔː] system of rules developed by government for regulating the behaviour of members of a community or country **administration** management of public or business affairs **to impose sth on sb** to use authority to force sb to accept sth **to retain** to keep sth **Plaid Cymru** [plæd ˈkʌmrɪ] Welsh nationalist party **to found** to start an organisation **referendum** vote or poll taken on an important issue by all the people in a country or region **vote** formal indication of choice in an election or referendum **electorate** [ɪˈlektərət] people who have the right to vote in an election **tax** money that has to be paid to the government **election** organised process of choosing by vote a person or group for an official position or political office

Regional Perspectives

| **Working with the language** | Based on the information in Milestones of Devolution, write a paragraph on devolution using the passive voice.
Start with: England and Wales were united by the 1536 Act of Union. |

Decisive Vote By Scots

Scotland's verdict was by no means unanimous but it was emphatic. Not only did 73.4 per cent of those who turned out back the creation of a Scottish parliament, but the Yes forces won handsome majorities in every local authority area. […]

As expected, support for home rule proved strongest on Clydeside and in the industrial belt stretching east of Glasgow. […]

Geography was important. Broadly speaking, the farther a part of the country was from the central lowland belt dominated by Glasgow, Edinburgh and Dundee, the less likely it was to vote overwhelmingly for home rule.

Highland, the Western Isles and Aberdeen cast more than 70 per cent of their vote for the new parliament but otherwise the Yes percentages in outlying and rural Scotland tended to be considerably smaller.

Turnout was lower than average in all the big cities – Aberdeen, Dundee, Edinburgh and Glasgow. […]

The low turnout suggests that national passions in Scotland were far from inflamed.

In every authority, the vote for tax-varying powers fell well short of the vote for a new parliament. […]

In general, prosperous areas seem to have been least keen to give the new parliament powers to tax.

The contrast with the 1979 referendum is striking. At that time only 51.6 per cent of voters backed the home-rule parliament then on offer. Last Thursday the corresponding figure was 74.3 per cent – a "swing" towards home rule of more than 21 per cent. […]

The Weekly Telegraph, October 8, 1997

'Your mother and I would like to give you the chance to break away and start raising your own revenue.'

---

vote formal indication of choice in an election or referendum **1 verdict** decision **2 unanimous** [juːˈnæ-nɪməs] with all in agreement on a decision **3 emphatic** [ɪmˈfætɪk] forceful **4/5 to turn out** to attend **5 to back** to support **7 force** here: group **8/9 local authority** local government having the power to make decisions **12 Clydeside** area around Glasgow on River Clyde **13 belt** here: narrow region **21/22 overwhelming** [ˌəʊvəˈwelmɪŋ] very strong **23/24 to cast a vote** to give a vote **26 outlying** remote **rural** of the countryside **27 to tend to** to be likely to **29 turnout** number of people who attend sth **35 inflamed** (adj) angry or excited **37 tax** money that has to be paid to the government **40 prosperous** [ˈ---] rich, successful **41 to be keen to do sth** to be enthusiastic about doing sth **45 striking** (adj) attracting attention because of being extreme **49 swing** here: move, significant change

Internet The Scotsman → http://www.scotsman.com

 Great Britain

How they voted

Voters were asked:
Q1: I agree that there should be a Scottish Parliament.
　: I do not agree that there should be a Scottish Parliament.
Q2: I agree that a Scottish Parliament should have tax powers.
　: I do not agree that a Scottish Parliament should have tax powers.

	Q 1		Q 2		%
	Yes %	No %	Yes %	No %	Turnout
Aberdeen	71.8	28.2	60.3	39.7	53.7
Dumfries & Galloway	60.7	39.3	48.8	51.2	63.4
Dundee	76.0	24.0	65.5	34.5	55.7
Edinburgh	71.9	28.1	62.0	38.0	60.1
Falkirk	80.0	20.0	69.2	30.8	63.7
Glasgow	83.6	16.4	75.0	25.0	51.6
Highland	72.6	27.4	62.0	38.0	60.3
Orkney	57.3	42.7	47.4	52.6	53.5
Scottish Borders	62.8	37.2	50.7	49.3	64.8
Shetland	62.4	37.6	51.6	48.4	51.5
West Dumbartonshire	84.7	15.3	74.7	25.3	63.7
Western Isles	79.4	20.6	68.4	31.6	55.8
SCOTLAND	**74.3**	**25.7**	**63.5**	**36.5**	**60.4**

Discussing the text
Comment on the regional variations in the referendum results in Scotland.

Regional Perspectives

The Welsh Decision

The referendum campaign in Wales may be over, and the Welsh assembly secured, albeit by the tiniest of margins (just 50.3% of the electorate bothered to vote at all), but the government's battle to convince the Welsh, and indeed parts of the Welsh Labour Party, that they have done the right thing is just beginning.

The divisions revealed in Wales by the result are nothing new. The abortive 1979 referendum, when Wales voted four to one against devolution, disclosed a country split three ways. Denis Balsom, a political scientist at the University of Wales, has classified these areas as Welsh-speaking Wales (stretching from the northwest counties down to Carmarthenshire): Welsh Wales (people in the former mining valleys of south Wales who feel Welsh but do not speak it) and British Wales (the rest, where most people are either English-born or work in English cities like Manchester or Bristol). By and large, 18 years later, the first two areas voted Yes and the third voted No (see map).

Despite the divided vote, the assembly will go ahead with elections in 1999, its work starting soon thereafter.

The Economist, September 27, 1997

'Darling, am I in favour of self rule?'

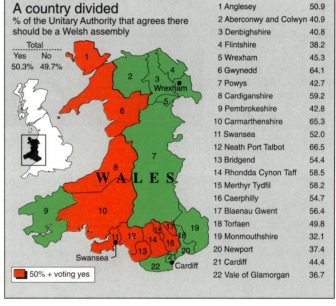

1 Anglesey	50.9	
2 Aberconwy and Colwyn	40.9	
3 Denbighshire	40.8	
4 Flintshire	38.2	
5 Wrexham	45.3	
6 Gwynedd	64.1	
7 Powys	42.7	
8 Cardiganshire	59.2	
9 Pembrokeshire	42.8	
10 Carmarthenshire	65.3	
11 Swansea	52.0	
12 Neath Port Talbot	66.5	
13 Bridgend	54.4	
14 Rhondda Cynon Taff	58.5	
15 Merthyr Tydfil	58.2	
16 Caerphilly	54.7	
17 Blaenau Gwent	56.4	
18 Torfaen	49.8	
19 Monmouthshire	32.1	
20 Newport	37.4	
21 Cardiff	44.4	
22 Vale of Glamorgan	36.7	

Discussing the text Comment on the geographical divisions revealed by the referendum in Wales.

Going beyond the text Using the information in both texts and referring to the map and the table of results, compare the election results in Scotland to those in Wales. How big a role does geography play?

---

2 to secure to obtain, to get **albeit** [ɔːlˈbiːɪt] although **3 tiny** very small **margin** amount **3/4 electorate** [ɪˈlektərət] the people who have the right to vote in an election **4 to bother to do sth** to take the time to do sth **9 abortive** unsuccessful **11 to disclose** to make sth known **split** divided **16 mining** the process of getting coal or other minerals from the ground

A United Kingdom?

How united will the Kingdom be after Tony Blair's radical reforms take hold?

One of the most highly centralized states in the world, a country which has always taken its unity for granted, is giving power back to each of the nations which make up the United Kingdom. The question, of course, is just how united the Kingdom will be once Blair has finished. [...]

Constitutional reform at home is certain to make Britain more European. At meetings in Brussels, Scottish and Welsh ministers will represent their nations inside a British delegation, just as the Bavarians do in West German delegations.

Most of the country seems to agree with Blair that devolution does not necessarily mean divorce. Popular support for full Scottish independence is stuck somewhere between a quarter and a third of the Scottish electorate and there's little evidence that Scotland is headed for secession just because it has voted for its own assembly. Ditto for Wales.

Blair's historic gamble is that devolution will strengthen, not weaken, the Union. If Europe's experience is any guide, giving power back to the Catalans or the Bavarians has reduced regional discontent, not made it worse. As for devolution's impact on British identity, it is bound to make complex loyalties still more so. The Scots will feel more Scottish, but that doesn't necessarily mean they will feel less British. All over Europe double, even triple loyalties are the order of the day.

The real question mark with the Blair revolution may be where it leaves the English. Already, English regions like the North-East, centred around Newcastle, are considering their own assemblies, if only to get power to compete with Scotland and Wales for foreign investment. The problem is that nobody quite knows what it means to be English anymore. Blacks and Asians call themselves British, never English. The white English thought they lived in an English state which just happened to include ethnic minorities and a Celtic fringe. Devolution awakens them to the new reality that they are just one people within a multinational federation.

Michael Ignatieff

Time, October 27, 1997

Multiple Loyalties: A Scottish "Aye" for devolution

2/3 to take sth for granted to be so familiar with sth that one no longer appreciates its full value **25 divorce** separation **26 to stick** to be fixed in one place and unable to move **28 electorate** people who have the right to vote in an election **29 to head for sth** to be likely to result in a particular situation **secession** [sɪˈseʃn] formal separation **30 ditto** [ˈdɪtəʊ] the same thing again **32 gamble** risky action or decision you take in the hope of gaining success **36 discontent** [ˌ--ˈ-] dissatisfaction **38 bound to do sth** certain to do sth **64 happened** here: *zufällig*

Regional Perspectives

Understanding the text

1. Why is Britain likely to become more European after constitutional reform?
2. Why are Scotland and Wales unlikely to move towards full independence?
3. What is the impact of devolution on national identity in England and in Scotland?

Going beyond the text

1. Despite the move towards a stronger European identity, why is national identity still so important within individual countries?
2. Where do other examples of nationalist movements exist around the world? What are possible causes of these movements?

Working with thematic vocabulary

Collect the words connected with *devolution* from the texts you have read and group them under the following headings. Include nouns, verbs and adjectives.

devolution	election	political party

Great Britain And Europe: Merry Old England And Brave New Europe

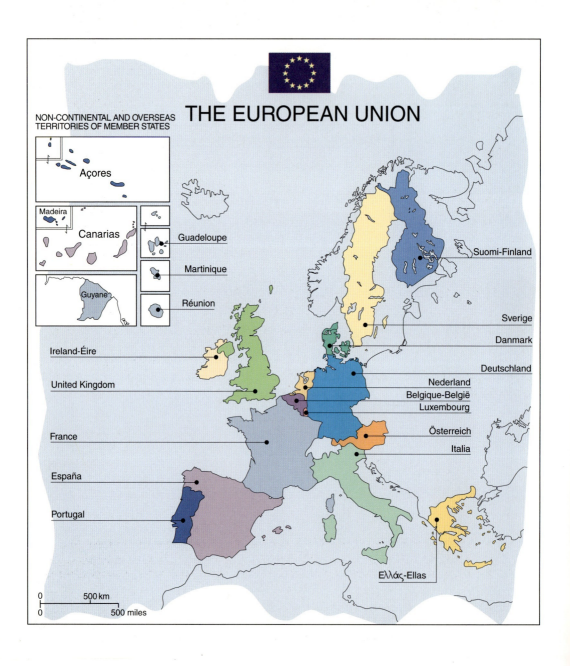

Merry Old England And Brave New Europe

Getting to know the perfect European

1. What nations are presently EU members?
2. What national stereotype is shown in each picture?
3. Which stylistic device does the cartoonist use to cause amusement?
4. Make a list of all the adjectives used in describing the different nationalities and find the corresponding nouns. For example: available – availability

Brit (infml, often derog) a British person **sober** not drunk; serious and sensible **humble** not proud **generous** ready to give freely **patient** able to accept delay or other unpleasant things without complaining

Great Britain And Europe

Pre-reading activity: Why do you think English is the most commonly taught language in Europe?

English Is The Most Commonly Taught Language In Europe

Britain may still be on the periphery of Europe as far as her European Union partners are concerned, but English is taking over as the Continent's most common language, according to statistics released in Brussels last week.

They show that almost 90 per cent of all youngsters are now being taught English as a second language, much to the chagrin of the French, who have discovered their language has been supplanted everywhere beyond its borders except in the institutions of the European Union.

Less than a third of non-French speaking children are now being taught French as their second language.

German comes a poor third – just 18 per cent learn it as a second language, followed by 8 per cent learning Spanish.

Even in primary schools, a quarter of European youngsters are taught English, with French being taught to just 4 per cent of non-Francophones.

The French government is so concerned that it is making strenuous efforts to sponsor language teaching, both in the EU applicant countries of eastern Europe and in the Far East. A recent gathering of Francophone nations found more than 100 where the language is spoken by more than a tiny minority.

The British are maintaining their reputation for not being able to speak foreign languages – the survey shows that the UK is alone among member states, except for Ireland, in not teaching primary school children a second language.

Even at secondary level it does not compete with the range of languages taught elsewhere, such as Finland, the Netherlands, and Luxembourg, where two or three extra languages are the norm.

The educational statistics indicate accelerating trends for children to start school earlier – most three-year-olds in many countries have already started schooling – and a doubling of the numbers entering higher education over the past two decades.

Stephen Bates

The Guardian Weekly, February 22, 1998

Understanding the text
1. What role do English, French, German and Spanish play as second languages taught at schools in the EU nations?
2. Why are France and Britain linguistic rivals?

Discussing the text
Which of the two foreign languages (English and French) you have been learning so far at school do you favour? Why?

---

1 periphery [pəˈrɪfəri] (fml) here: position on the outside of a political group **5 to release** to allow news, facts or information to be made known **8 chagrin** [ˈʃægrɪn; US ʃəˈgrɪn] feeling of disappointment at having made a mistake **10 to supplant** to replace **24 strenuous** [ˈstrenjuəs] *anstrengend* **effort** [ˈ--] use of much physical or mental energy to do sth **27 gathering** meeting of people **29 tiny** very small **30 to maintain** to cause sth to continue **30 reputation** *Ruf* **32 survey** *Überblick* **35/36 to compete with sb for sth** to try to win by defeating others **36 range** number of different things of the same general type **40 to indicate** to show **to accelerate** to make sth happen faster or earlier **45 decade** period of 10 years

Merry Old England And Brave New Europe

The Madness Of Metrication

A reader warns against the continuing European colonisation of our heritage ...

Sir: During the last two years the self-appointed metrication lobby in Europe has been able to impose, manipulate and reinforce its crusade to rid us of our traditional English systems of weights and measures, currency and culture. [...]

[Yet] we do *not* exist in a metric Universe. We *do* live in a Universe where there is order, but it is far more diverse and complex than can be squeezed and manipulated into multiples of ten! [...]

A brief look at several aspects of the world and life around us soon begins to illustrate our very non-metric existence. Within the Universe, we live in a solar system of nine planets. One earth year is 365 1/4 days, whilst on Mars it is 687 days. Everyone on earth uses a 12-month, seven-day week, with a 24-hour day/night period made up of 3,600 seconds – nothing very metric there!

We are greatly influenced in our time, weather and seasons by the moon, which orbits us approximately every 27 1/2 days causing our tides to change every 13 hours or so - no room for a 10-hour clock in these variants!

Roger Dykes   This England, Winter 1997

Understanding the text

1. How does the speaker feel about losing the traditional English measurements?
2. To what extent is the speaker critical of our modern times?
3. Which words in the text clearly illustrate the author's point of view?
4. Why does the author think of metrication as madness?

Going beyond the text

What else may get lost together with the old English measurements?

Working with the language

Find other verbs in the previous text whose nouns take the suffix "-ment." For example: measure - measurement; appointed - appointment; reinforce - reinforcement ...

---

heritage ['herɪtɪdʒ] things that have been passed on from earlier generations **1 self-appointed** *selbst ernannt* **2 metrication** act of measuring according to the metric system **3 to impose sth on sb** to try forcefully to make sb accept sth **to reinforce** [riːɪnˈfɔːs] to strengthen **crusade** *Kreuzzug* **4 to rid sb of sth** to make sb free of sth that causes trouble **5 currency** system of money used in a country **9 diverse** [daɪˈvɜːs] of different kinds **10 to squeeze sth into sth** to force sth into a limited space **12 brief** short **22 to orbit** to follow the path of a planet round another body **23 approximately** about **24 tide** regular rise and fall in the level of the sea **25 variant** ['veəriənt] sth that differs from other things or from a standard

Measure For Measure

They did away with stones and pounds
And I was devastated,
For I spent many weary hours
Just being indoctrinated.

5 With feet and inches, yards and chains,
And rods and poles and perches,
The pages of my table books
Are a goldmine for researchers.

Upon request, I could recite
10 Like a spirit invocation,
The weights and measures, pounds and pence,
With little hesitation.

I knew how many pence there were
In ten pounds four and seven,
15 And I could buy a pair of shoes
For fourteen and eleven.

The friendly corner grocery shop
Had cheeses flat or round;
With a wire to cut a quarter off
20 If you didn't want a pound.

My recipe books were sprinkled with
Handfuls and cups and pinches,
And spices using just a touch
And pastry rolled in inches.

25 But we are more efficient now,
Tables are out of date;
A pocket gadget's all we need
To help us calculate.

The supermarket shelves are filled
30 With packets ready made;
You just add water to the cake
With eggs (all battery laid!)

We take our well-filled trolleys
And wheel them to the scanner;
35 Then we're told: "Have a nice day"
– in the insincerest manner!
Margaret Walker

This England, Winter 1997

Discussing the texts

List all the old English measurements mentioned in the poem. Compare this list with your pre-reading findings from "The Madness of Metrication." Which measurements had you never heard of?

---

2 to devastate ['devəsteɪt] (infml, often passive) to cause sb extreme distress **3 weary** ['wɪəri] causing one to feel tired **4 to indoctrinate** [-'---] to cause sb to have a particular belief **5 chain** old measurement of length **6 rod, pole, perch** here: 3 terms used for expressing a length of 5.5 yards **7 table book** *Tabellenbuch* **8 researcher** [rɪ'sɜːtʃə] sb who studies sth carefully in order to discover new information **9 upon request** if asked for **to recite** to say sth from memory **10 invocation** cf to invoke: to make sth appear by magic **12 hesitation** *Zögern* **19 wire** *Draht* **21 recipe** ['resəpi] *Rezept* **to sprinkle with** here: to cover with in small quantities **22 pinch** as much as can be held between the tips of the thumb and first finger **23 spice** substance used in cooking for producing a special taste **24 pastry** ['peɪstri] *Teig* **25 efficient** able to work well without wasting time and resources **27 pocket gadget** ['gædʒɪt] here: *Taschenrechner* **33 trolley** (Brit) here: *Einkaufswagen* **34 to wheel** to push a vehicle **36 insincere** [ɪnsɪn'sɪə(r)] not honest, not true

Internet Metrication → http://home.clara.net/brianp/index.html

Britain And Europe

How is the relationship between GB and Europe portrayed here?

When Britain joined the European Economic Community in 1973, many continental Europeans looked forward to the prospect of three countries, rather than just two, leading the enterprise. Smaller member states, especially, looked to Britain to weaken the Franco-German hegemony and occasionally speak up for their interests. Britain's economy responded to the European challenge, but not its politicians. For most of the past 25 years, Britain has shown that it does not share Germany's and France's belief in a more united Europe. Whatever the results of the elections for the European Parliament, Britain has remained in the slow lane.
Given the original aims of the European Union (EU) as a means to bind together the continent's two biggest powers, and defuse their historical rivalry, the hope that Britain could play an equal role with France and Germany may always have been unrealistic. But this did not make Britain's marginalisation inevitable. Many EU members have sadly concluded that Britain has so far played its hand badly.
When John Major replaced Margaret Thatcher as prime minister in November 1990, Britain's reputation in the EU grew. In March 1991 he declared that Britain should be at the heart of Europe. Support from Germany's Helmut Kohl helped Mr. Major to win arguments at the Maastricht Summit. After the Danes voted against the Maastricht Treaty in 1992, Mr. Major seemed more willing to calm down his party's Eurosceptics than his European partners.
Meanwhile the single market is about to give birth to monetary union and the great project of a federal Europe, of which the euro is a crucial

---

5 enterprise project; business activity **7 hegemony** [ˈhedʒɪməni] (fml) control and leadership, esp by one country over others within a group **8 to respond to sth** to react quickly or favourably to sth **9 challenge** *Herausforderung* **14 lane** *(Straßen)spur* **16 means** (sing or pl) method **17 to defuse** to reduce possible danger in a difficult situation **18 rivalry** [ˈraɪvəlri] competition between two people wanting the same **21 marginalisation** [ˌmɑːdʒɪnəlaɪˈzeɪʃən] act of making sb/sth become or feel less important **inevitable** [ɪnˈevɪtəbl] *unvermeidbar* **23 to play one's hand badly** to fail to use one's chance fully **32 to calm (sb) down** to make sb become calm **33 Eurosceptics** people who are sceptical about a united Europe **36 crucial** [ˈkruːʃl] very important

Great Britain And Europe

step, is on its way. The victory of Tony Blair's New Labour Party marks the end of almost two decades of British hostility towards Brussels and a fresh start in Europe for Britain, working with other members as a partner, not as an opponent, thus getting a better deal for Britain. Tony Blair, Britain's new pro-European prime minister, likes to refer to the notion of the "People's Europe" and does not hesitate to show his enthusiasm for the European Union. Nevertheless, he is ambivalent to the idea of a single currency and does not really want to sell the euro to a sceptical British public. However, he is already under business pressure to join the European Monetary Union (EMU) at the outset in 1999, no matter how much the Britons question the idea. Once a single currency is introduced in the European Union in January 1999, Britain will definitely not be in the first wave of monetary union, having chosen to remain on the sidelines first and wait for a strong euro, i.e. a currency with credibility. According to Britain's finance minister, Gordon Brown, Britain would join the single currency if and when economic conditions were right, but only after the referendum, which would not take place before the year 2002.*

Understanding the text

1. What role has Britain played in the EU up to now?
2. What is Britain's new position in the EU under Tony Blair?
3. Describe in your own words Britain's attitude towards the European Monetary Union.

Going beyond the text

1. Think of reasons that may be responsible for Britain's scepticism towards Europe.
2. What is your personal attitude towards a single European currency?

Working with the language

Find all the idiomatic expressions used in the text and suggest adequate idiomatic translations in German.
(eg: l. 14 "Britain has remained in the slow lane" = *Großbritannien verharrt in Warteposition*)

---

39 decade period of 10 years **hostility** agressive feelings or behaviour **41/42 opponent** [-'---] person who is against another person **42 to get a better deal for sb** *für jdn mehr herausholen* **44 notion** idea, belief **45 to hesitate** to be slow to act because one feels uncertain or unwilling **46 enthusiasm** [ɪnˈθjuːzɪæzəm] *Begeisterung* **47 ambivalent** [-'---] having mixed feelings about sb/sth **51 outset** start, beginning **52 Britons** the British people **to question** to feel doubt about sth **55 wave** here: movement, process **58 credibility** *Glaubwürdigkeit* **61 referendum** vote taken on an important decision by all the people of a country

Merry Old England And Brave New Europe

Pre-reading activity

1. What do you know about BSE?
2. How did the BSE epidemic in Great Britain affect your family's consumer mentality?

Farmers Philosophical Over Latest Blow

Mr. Wharfe, a farmer for 35 years, enjoys his job but is frustrated at the way the BSE crisis has developed – and at the drop in his income.

"I've always maintained that the chances of getting BSE are like a blind man looking in a dark room for a black hat that isn't there," he said. The fact that scientists have now decided that 1 per cent of calves will inherit BSE from their mothers is neither here nor there; things cannot get much worse than they already are: the pretty little black and white calf will fetch just £100 when she goes to Chelford market in a couple of weeks. A year ago she would have sold for £250.

Mr. Wharfe had one case of BSE in his herd three years ago, but has been clear since. "There were 3,000 cases a week then, when BSE was at its height. Now there are about 200. The compensation system worked very well and made sure that nothing could slip through the net.

"Farmers realise there is a problem but the scare has been out of all proportion to the risk. We are aware of the risk in society of things like drugs, Aids and crime. But the risk of BSE is so small it's barely worth a mention."

Mr. Wharfe, needless to say, has not given up beef. He is deeply worried by the nation's shift to vegetarianism, a shift which has galloped ahead during the last year of confusion and panic.

"BSE is on the way out. If this had blown up three years ago, it would have been much easier to have understood the furor that has been created. It seems tragic when we were getting on top of the situation.

"Over the years we have had lots of eradication schemes in agriculture. Tuberculosis was eradicated in the fifties, brucellosis in the seventies. People possibly had more to fear from those two than they will ever have to fear from BSE.

"The problem has been hyped up out of all proportion. We are being asked to do the impossible and prove a negative. But everything we consume has an element of risk, and beef is no exception."

David Ward

The Guardian Weekly, August 18, 1996

Understanding the text

1. How was Wharfe personally affected by the BSE crisis in Britain?
2. What does Wharfe think about the BSE problem?
3. Why does he himself not share the common worries?

---

2 BSE (abbr; also infml **mad cow disease**) bovine spongiform encephalopathy **3 drop** reduction, fall **3 income** payment for work **4 to maintain** to insist that sth is the case **8 calf** (pl calves) young cow **to inherit** [-'--] to have qualities similar to the parents **18 at its height** highest degree of sth **18/19 compensation** here: *Wiedergutmachung* **20 to slip through the net** to escape from sth that has been organized to catch it **21 scare** sudden feeling of fear **25 barely** hardly; *kaum* **28 shift** change of position or direction **to gallop** ['--] to move rapidly **31 to blow up** to start suddenly and with force **33 furor** ['fjʊərɔː(r)] (Brit furore) display of great anger or excitement shown by a number of people **36 eradication** [ɪˌrædɪˈkeɪʃn] cf to eradicate: to put an end to sth; to destroy completely **38 brucellosis** disease harming humans and animals that was caused by the brucella bacteria **41 to hype sth up** (infml) to exaggerate the importance of sth in order to get maximum public attention for it

Great Britain And Europe

British Farmers Demonstrate Against EU Policies

treachery [ˈtretʃəri] behaviour that involves betraying sb/sth, esp secretly

Merry Old England And Brave New Europe

Discussing the photographs

1. Which of the British farmers' slogans would Mr. Wharfe support? Why?
2. Comment on the slogan "No Mass-Trick Treachery." What effect does this play on words have?
3. What makes the farmers want a referendum now? What would this referendum be about?

Would It Have Been Better If We Hadn't Joined The EU?

On January 1, 1973, the UK entered the European Community. But even 25 years later, the argument about Britain's membership is a long way from being settled.

YES
says
Bill Jamieson,
Sunday Telegraph
Economics Editor

Bill Jamieson stood as a UK Independence Party candidate at the general election.

[…] The acid test is surely this: have we become more European over these 25 years? Do we aspire to a more European view, or share more than we did her politics, customs and manners? 5

In some respects we have grown closer. We enjoy the speedier processing as EU nationals at airports. We jostle as keenly as our neighbours for Euro hand-outs. We still yearn for the cafe chic of Paris, the technical proficiency of the 10 Germans, the spontaneity of Italy. We seek to emulate classical European standards in architecture, the arts and social mores.

But in outlook we have not become noticeably more European. We are not filled with a sense 15

---

1 acid test (sing) test that gives final proof of the value or worth of sth/sb **3 to aspire to sth** to have a strong desire to achieve sth **8 to jostle for sth** to compete with other people in a forceful manner in order to gain sth **keen** eager; *eifrig* **9 hand-out** money, food or clothes given free to a person in need **9 to yearn for sth** to desire sth strongly **10 proficiency** skilled and expert way of doing sth **11 spontaneity** [spɒntə'neɪti] quality of doing or saying sth because of a sudden impulse from within **to seek** (fml; pt, pp sought [sɔːt]) here: to try to get **12 to emulate sb** ['---] (fml) to try to do as well as or better than sb **14 noticeable** easily seen; clear

of European "destiny" or "mission." We are unimpressed with European political institutions, returning members to the European parliament with barely a third of the electorate bothering to vote. We recoil from federal union.

We hoot at the bureaucracy of Brussels. We resent the elitism and arrogance of the EU's political class and we do not (to put it mildly) defer to the official language of the EU more than we did in 1973. We have not, in short, fundamentally changed our world view: if anything our cultural cross-over from beyond Europe is all the greater.

And in linguistic and cultural terms, in the realm of popular music and fashion and style, in the growth in the use of the English language, there has been more of an Anglicisation of the Continent rather than a Europeanisation of Britain.

There is now, of course, "Le Chunnel." But the divide between Britain and the Continent is as wide as ever. We are still Anglo Saxons, with a distinctive and singular view of how the EU should evolve, and that view is fundamentally and implacably at odds with the goal of economic, monetary and political union.

How, then, should we celebrate these 25 years? For the political class and officials there will be summits and meetings of EU leaders; at town hall level telegram exchanges of congratulation with our civic twins. But what will we really do at heart? Sigh with helpless resignation, I suspect, and yearn for something less depressing.

The Weekly Telegraph, No. 337, 1997

Understanding the text

1. To what extent has Britain become more European?
2. List all the arguments Jamieson puts forward in order to show that Britain has nevertheless not been Europeanized.

Analysing the text

Comment on the sentence structure of Jamieson's arguments. What effect does this sentence structure have on the reader?

Translate

Lines 34–47.

---

16 destiny fate; *Schicksal* **19 barely** hardly; *kaum* **electorate** [-'---] all the electors considered as a group **to bother** ['bɒðə(r)] to take the time or trouble to do sth **20 to recoil from sth** [rɪˈkɔɪl] to move one's body quickly away from sth with a feeling of fear **21 to hoot at** to make noises showing disapproval or contempt **22 to resent** [-'-] to feel bitter or angry about sth **elitism** (often derog) attitude or behaviour of sb who considers they belong to an elite **24 to defer to sth** to show respect for sth **25/26 fundamentally** in the most important or essential aspects **27 cultural cross-over** process of developing or changing from one type of culture to another **28 all the greater** *umso größer* **29 realm** [relm] field of activity or interest **37 distinctive** made different from others **38 to evolve** to develop naturally and gradually **39 implacable** [ɪmˈplækəbl] that cannot be changed or satisfied **to be at odds with sb/sth** to disagree with **goal** aim, object of one's efforts **43 summit** here: meeting between the heads of two or more governments **45 civic twins** here: *Partnerstädte* **46 to sigh** *seufzen* **46/47 to suspect** [-'-] to believe

Merry Old England And Brave New Europe

NO
says
Sir Roy Denman,
who helped negotiate Britain's 1973 entry.

Sir Roy Denman was a member of the Civil Service team which negotiated British entry in 1970–72. He is the author of Missed Chances: Britain and Europe in the 20th Century *(Cassell, 1996).*

Few institutions can ever have provoked as much questioning as the European Community. Back on January 1, 1973, the question – was Britain right to join? – was being asked with as much intensity as it still is today.

To join an organisation that was already 16 years old was hardly a rash and impulsive action. Indeed, Britain joined only after long and bitter debate. But the specific questions being raised on New Year's Day 25 years ago can now, with the benefit of hindsight, be easily answered. So what were they?

It was claimed then that cheap foreign imports would depress the British standard of living. But Britain today is booming. This year both Conservative and Labour politicians have made much of it. Compared with 1972 the country is two thirds richer. [...]

Ah, say the sceptics, but we still have to pay crippling sums into the EU budget. In fact, our net contribution amounts to £1 per head per week. A modest sum for a guarantee of no new European war and free access to a huge continental market. The anti-Europeans 25 years ago were worried about Britain's role on the world stage. They feared that entry would damage our links with the Commonwealth. But the Commonwealth today is alive, well and even expanding.

Our entry, they said, would mean the end of our special relationship with the United States. This argument is hardly borne out by the help the Americans gave us in the Falklands war, or the help we gave them in the Gulf war. [...]

Despite all the fuss created by Euro-sceptical politicians, the British public seems to be clear what it thinks. A referendum on membership in 1975 showed a two thirds majority in favour. Only one third of voters want to leave now.

But if anniversaries are occasions to reflect on the past they should also prompt a look at the future. In a year's time most members of the EU will be embarking on a single currency. Why has Britain been so lukewarm and indefinite about joining it? [...] For a customs union to exist, it is necessary to allow free movement of goods. For a customs union to be a reality, it is necessary to allow free movement of persons. For a customs union to be stable it is necessary to maintain free exchange of currency and stable exchange rate within the union.

When there is free movement of goods, persons and capital in any area, diverse economic policies

---

7 rash (adj) acting or done without careful consideration of the possible results **11 benefit** advantage **hindsight** [aɪ] understanding of a situation or an event only after it has occurred **14 to depress** to make sth less active **19/20 crippling** (adj) here: extremely large and damaging **21 contribution** [--'--] money given to an organization **to amount to sth** to have as a total **22 modest** *bescheiden* **23 access to sth** ['--] way into sth **26 entry** here: act of becoming a member of sth **link** connection **28 to expand** [-'-] to make sth greater in size or number **31 to bear sth out** (pt bore; pp borne) to support sth; to show sth is true **34 fuss** display of excitement, worry or enthusiasm over sth unimportant **39 anniversary** date that is exactly a year or a number of years after an event **40 to prompt** to cause (a feeling or an action) **42 to embark on sth** to start sth new or difficult **43 lukewarm** here: not eager or enthusiastic **indefinite** not clearly defined **44 customs union** *Zollunion* **48 stable** (adj) firmly established **to maintain** to cause sth to continue **49 exchange rate** *Wechselkurs* **52 capital** here: all the wealth owned by a business **diverse** of different kinds

cannot be pursued. To assure uniformity of policy some mechanism is required. The greater the interference of the state in economic life, the greater must be the political integration.
This is the track we are on. We are half way. Do we want to continue? If we stop, we could negotiate a free trade arrangement with Europe. But the conditions would be humiliating – acceptance of all regulations on trade negotiated in Brussels without being able to participate in any of the decision-making.
If we do continue, then it is via an economic and monetary union towards some form of political union. In this, a fullhearted participation by Britain could enable it to play a major role in Europe and in the world.
But this choice needs to be spelt out to the British people. They, not politicians or bureaucrats, need to decide. […]
So the 25th anniversary of our entry into Europe is both a success and a challenge. On how we answer that challenge depends the future of this country in the 21st century.

The Weekly Telegraph, No. 337, 1997

Understanding the text

1. What did the Eurosceptics predict 25 years ago when Britain finally joined the EU?
2. What has now become of these prophecies?
3. What are Denman's arguments for Britain's embarking on a single European currency?
4. What kind of appeal does he make at the end of his argument?

Working with the texts

Write a dialogue between a British Eurosceptic and a Europhile about the issue of joining the EU as it might have taken place 25 years ago. Use the information given in the text (lines 13–33).

Selling The Euro To The British

Seventy-six percent of the British people think they should decide about Britain's entry into the EMU themselves. However, the British government has already begun trying to sell the euro to the British so that the electorate will vote 'yes' in a referendum.

The New Statesman, a British political news magazine, asked an advertising agency to start the job the government will soon have to take on: sell the euro to the Brits.
Here are some examples of what they devised:

---

53 to pursue (fml) to do; to take part in sth **assure** to make sth certain **55 interference** [--'--] *Einmischung* **57 track** direction followed **58/59 to negotiate** [nɪˈgəʊʃɪeɪt] to try to reach agreement by discussion **60 humiliating** (adj) [-'----] *erniedrigend* **62 to participate** to take part in **69 to spell sth out** to make sth clear and easy to understand **74 challenge** *Herausforderung*

Merry Old England And Brave New Europe

DRIVE A HARDER BARGAIN.
VOTE YES TO THE SINGLE CURRENCY.

U.K.
£8,145

GERMANY
£6,782

ITALY
£6,409

IN A COMMON MARKET A COMMON CURRENCY IS COMMON SENSE.

THE THREE MOST POWERFUL CURRENCIES IN THE WORLD.

THE DOLLAR, THE YEN AND THE ONE BRITAIN HASN'T JOINED YET.

IN A COMMON MARKET A COMMON CURRENCY IS COMMON SENSE.

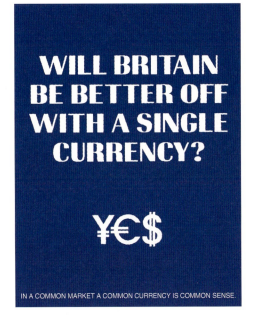

WILL BRITAIN BE BETTER OFF WITH A SINGLE CURRENCY?

¥€$

IN A COMMON MARKET A COMMON CURRENCY IS COMMON SENSE.

Discussing the advertisements — Which of the three adverts do you find the most convincing? Why?

to drive a hard bargain [ˈbɑːgən] (idm) to argue aggressively and insist on the best possible deal or price

Internet The Euro → http://europa.eu.int/euro/html/entry.html

A Modern Britain, With America And In Europe

London – The British people this month elected a new government with a decisive mandate to modernize Britain. The world in which we conduct our diplomacy is changing rapidly. Trade between countries is accelerating much faster than growth within them. People travel more. Television and the Internet mean that our knowledge of each other is much deeper than before. Nightly we are presented with images on our television screens that we cannot mutely ignore.

Foreign policy is no esoteric game. It impacts directly on our peoples' lives, jobs, concerns. Engagement in the wider world isn't optional; it is essential. Now more than ever, isolationism or insularity would be self-defeating.

Last week I set out the goals of Britain's foreign policy.

First, Britain's security will remain founded on NATO. NATO will grow, and change, and Russia will have a voice, but not a veto. A strong alliance means greater security for all.

Second, our prosperity depends on vigorous free trade and healthy investment flows. Britain is the largest investor in America, and America the largest in Britain – America invests more in my country than in all Asia. A million Americans work in the United States for British firms. We shall work to create still greater links and synergies, and more open markets elsewhere. British foreign policy will reflect that.

Third, no government can today ignore the effects of global phenomena such as climate change. Getting firm agreements to protect climate, oceans and forests won't be easy, given the differing needs of countries at different stages of development, but I am determined to try.

Fourth, I believe that we cannot check in our consciences at the conference room door. The British people have a deep sense of fairness. Like Americans, they are determined not only that their society should remain open and democratic but also that others should share the freedoms they enjoy. [...]

Finally, Britain under New Labour will work much more closely with our partners in the European Union. I see no contradiction between close partnership with the United States and wholehearted involvement in Europe. On the contrary, with Britain back in a leading role, we can better influence European debate, and so strengthen transatlantic partnership.

For too long, Britain has stood on the sideline in Europe. The new government's positive approach brings better prospects of achieving the European Union we want: deeper and wider, with a vibrant single market generating more jobs; a warm welcome for new members from among our neighbors to the East; and the confidence and cohesion to play a greater role across the world.

Robin Cook
(The writer is the British foreign secretary.)
International Herald Tribune, May 21, 1997

---

2 decisive [dɪ'saɪsɪv] producing a particular or definite result **3/4 to conduct** [-'-] to direct or manage sth **5 accelerate** [ək'selərent] to happen or make sth happen faster **10 mute** silent **12 to impact on sth** (esp US) to have an effect on sth **13 concern** worry, anxiety **14 optional** that may be chosen or not, as one wishes **15 essential** important **16 insularity** [--'---] state of having no interest in or contact with people from outside one's own country **self-defeating** (adj) likely to achieve the opposite of what is intended **17 to set out** to present ideas, facts, etc in an organized way, in speech or writing **goal** aim, target **21 veto** ['viːtəʊ] right to say no **22 alliance** [-'--] association between countries **23 prosperity** state of being financially successful **vigorous** [vɪgərəs] strong, active, full of energy **29 link** connection **30 synergy** combined effect of two or more things that exeeds the sum of their individual parts **36 differing** (adj) not the same **37 to be determined to do sth** [dɪ'tɜːmɪnd] having made a firm decision to do sth **38 to check sth in** to leave sth (that is to be transported) **39 conscience** ['kɒnʃəns] *Gewissen* **49 wholehearted** (adj) without doubts; full and complete **involvement** act of taking part in sth **55 prospect** chance or hope that sth will happen **57 vibrant** [aɪ] full of life and energy; strong and powerful **to generate** to make sth exist or occur **59/60 confidence** *Vertrauen* **60 cohesion** [kəʊ'hiːʒn] state of sticking together

Merry Old England And Brave New Europe 115

Understanding the text
1. In what ways has our modern world changed?
2. Explain the five goals of Britain's new foreign policy in your own words. Write an eye-catching headline for each of the five goals.
3. What is Britain's new attitude towards Europe?

Translate
Lines 45–61.

Hilaire Belloc's View

Hilaire Belloc (1870–1953) lived most of his life in Britain, where he wrote many works of prose and verse. Belloc served as a member of parliament from 1906–1910. Over the next thirty years, Belloc wrote dozens of titles on varied subjects including poetry, fiction, political and social commentary, and military science.

'Except for the pride and honour of belonging to a great kingdom, to be a citizen of a small one seems to me to have all the advantages. In a great kingdom you have to pay heavy taxes. You are made falsely concerned with men whom you never see, and in doings far distant, which you do not understand; you bear on your shoulders the burden of millions, and you must suffer a capital city, which will be a sink of crime. Your rulers will grow rich by deceit – for a very large community can always be deceived: nothing about you will be real, and the mass of your fellow-citizens will be desperately poor. For it is the nature of large communities to separate into strata and for the mass to grow indignant.'
Hilaire Belloc

The Cruise of the "Nona," 1925

Understanding the text
Why is Belloc against large communities?

Going beyond the text
A true European would try to make Belloc change his mind. Write down his arguments.

---

1 honour good reputation **3 false** here: not real **4 to be concerned with** to have a connection with or a responsibility for **5 to bear** [beə(r)] (pt bore; pp borne) to carry **burden** responsibility that is not wanted **6 sink** Abflussbecken, Spülbecken **7 deceit** [dɪˈsiːt] cf to deceive: täuschen **9 desperate** [ˈdespərət] verzweifelt **10 stratum** [ˈstrɑːtəm] (pl **strata**) level or class of a society **11 indignant** [-'-] having or showing angry surprise because one believes that one has been treated unfairly

Great Britain And Europe

Cartoonists' Views

Working with the cartoons Compare the messages of the two cartoons.

Merry Old England And Brave New Europe

An Interview With Britain's Prime Minister

Time: *Britain has a record of missing the boat in Europe. Isn't that happening again with EMU?*
Blair: There was a great deal of hesitation (under the last government) about what Britain's role in relation to Europe should be. But there is no doubt at all so far as this government is concerned: we want to be a key, leading player in Europe. This does not mean you take positions contrary to your national interest in order to do that, but it does mean that we will get the best out of Europe for Britain. The reason I want to be a leading player is that I want to change Europe, which is far too hamstrung by bureaucracy and regulation. The Common Agricultural Policy is frankly a disgrace and must change. These are things we can achieve if we are in Europe. Obviously monetary union is the big project for most of the other countries in Europe. But we have to be in there raising the standard for people in Europe. There are two types of Europe: there is a people's Europe or a bureaucrats' Europe. We should be in there fighting on behalf of the European consumer. […]

Time: *What is Britain's position now on participation in European Economic and Monetary Union?*
Blair: Our position is very clear: there is no insuperable constitutional barrier to our joining a monetary union, but we think it is a question of whether our economic interest is served. Because the British position in the [economic] cycle is different from that of other European economies, it's unlikely that we will go into the first wave, but we will keep our options open. That freedom is best for us, but I understand why other countries see [joining the single currency] as a huge priority fo them. […]

Time: *And what about the British role in the world?*
Blair: A great British characteristic is to be open and outward-looking. British foreign policy is about being pivotal. We are not going to have the largest army in the world any more. We've not got an empire, but we have a series of

---

1 record ['--] sth known but not always written down about the past of sb/sth **4 hesitation** feeling of uncertainty with the consequence of being slow to speak or act **7 doubt** [daʊt] feeling of not being certain or not believing sth **7/8 as far as sth is concerned** to the extent that sb/sth is involved or affected **10 contrary to** (prep) in opposition to sth; against sth **14/15 hamstrung** (adj) prevented from working efficiently **15 bureaucracy** [bjʊəˈrɔkrəsi] *Bürokratie* **16 frankly** (adv) speaking honestly **16/17 disgrace** state in which one has lost honour or the respect of others; shame **18 to achieve** to succeed in doing sth **obviously** (adv) *offensichtlich* **21 to raise** to lift or move sth to a higher level **24 on behalf of** in the interests of sb **24/25 consumer** person who buys goods or uses services **26/27 participation** action of taking part in sth **30 insuperable** [-'----] that cannot be overcome **32 serve sb/sth** (esp passive) to provide sb/sth with a useful or necessary service **36 option** power or freedom of choosing; choice **39 priority** sth that is regarded as more important than others **44 pivotal** [ˈpɪvətl] of great importance because other things depend on it; central

Great Britain And Europe

How willingly is the lion leaping through the EU hoop?

relationships which, if we use them correctly, will make us a pivotal country – whether it is our relations with the United States, or inside Europe or within the Commonwealth and the U.N. All these things come under the rubric of using the strength of our history to build the future. We cannot pretend that the Empire is back because it isn't. My generation has moved on beyond all that. My generation has come to terms with its history. When I see the pageantry in Britain I think that's great, but it does not define where Britain is today. The whole idea of a modern British identity is not to displace the past, but to honor it by applying its best characteristics to today's world.

Time, October 27, 1997

Understanding the text

1. Describe Britain's new function in Europe.
2. What is Britain's view on taking part in the European Monetary Union?
3. What must a modern British identity be based upon, according to Tony Blair?

Working with the language

List all the words Blair uses which give a positive and optimistic outlook on life and the world in general.

Translate

Lines 42–68.

---

51 rubric ['--] (fml) title, instruction or rule printed in a different style from the rest **52 strength** here: the good qualities or abilities that a person or a thing has **54/55 to pretend** to make oneself appear to be sth **58 beyond** (prep) to the further side of sth **59/60 to come to terms with sth** to accept sth unpleasant over a period of time **61 pageantry** ['pædʒəntri] display and ceremony **66 to displace** to take the place of **67 to honor sth** (Brit **honour**) to show great respect for sth **to apply sth to sth** to make use of sth as relevant

Merry Old England And Brave New Europe

Education And Training: Tackling Unemployment In The European Job Market

The search for employment is becoming an increasingly uphill struggle in Europe. Employers are very demanding and look for staff with good qualifications and sound experience. The European Union is well aware of the problem and offers training and education programmes to improve your skills, brighten up your CV and better equip you for the labour market. The Union offers you an opportunity to take advantage of the accelerating pace of technological change rather than become a victim of it.

A young person is twice as likely to be unemployed as an older person. One in five longterm unemployed workers is under 25 years of age. Avoid becoming one of these statistics! Get up and go for it: explore what Europe has to offer in the way of education and training! Travel broadens the mind, so look out for the possibilities that will help you get ahead.

> **United Kingdom**
>
> **Socrates**
> UK Erasmus Student Grants Council
> The University Research and Development Building Canterbury
> Kent CT2 7PD
> Tel. (01227) 76 2712 - 74 4000 ext. 3673
>
> **Leonardo da Vinci**
> Department of Education and Employment
> Higher Education and Employment Division
> Sanctuary Buildings
> Great Smith Street
> London SW1P 3 BT
> Tel. (0 171) 925 53 06 - 925 5254
>
> **Youth for Europe**
> British Council Youth Exchange Centre
> 10 Spring Gardens
> London SW1A 2BN
> Tel. (0171) 389 4030

I. Socrates

The programme was launched in 1995 and now extends to the 15 Member States of the European Union plus Norway, Iceland and Liechtenstein.

Who can participate?
Socrates is open to students at all levels and in all types of education (day courses, adult education courses, etc.), schools at all levels, teachers, educational advisers, political decision-makers at all levels – local, regional or national – associations, organizations and societies engaged in education-related matters.

The funds available
For 1995-99, ECU 850 million has been allocated for the entire programme.

II. Leonardo da Vinci

The Leonardo programme was launched on 6 December 1994 and is based on Article 127 of the Treaty. It applies to all the Member States of the European Union, plus Norway, Iceland and Liechtenstein. It will also be open to the associated countries of Central and Eastern Europe and Cyprus and Malta.

---

to tackle to deal with or overcome sth difficult **2 struggle** difficult task requiring great effort **3 demanding** (adj) making others work hard **staff** all the workers employed in a business **4 sound** (adj) full and complete **7 skill** ability to do sth well **to brighten sth up** to make sth brighter or more hopeful **CV** curriculum vitae; *Lebenslauf* **10 to accelerate** [əkˈseləreɪt] to happen or make sth happen faster **pace** the speed at which sth progresses, develops, changes **11 victim** *Opfer* **12 likely** (adj) probable or expected **19 to get ahead** to progress **21 to launch** [lɔːntʃ] to start sth **22 to extend to** to make sth larger **31 to be engaged in** to take part in **33 fund** sum of money made available for a particular purpose **34/35 to allocate sth to sb/sth** to distribute sth officially to sb/sth for a special purpose **35 entire** (adj) whole, complete **39 treaty** *Vertrag* **41/42 to associate** to connect people or things because they occur together

Great Britain And Europe

Who may participate?

Leonardo da Vinci is open to all local, regional or national groups interested in vocational training in Europe. Pilot projects, exchanges and other placements are open to young people undergoing training, young workers in continuous training, firms and groups of firms (especially small businesses), language teachers and all public bodies.

The funds available
For 1995-99, ECU 620 million has been made available to implement the programme.

III. 'Youth For Europe'

This five-year programme was adopted in March 1995. It succeeds two other programmes of the same name. It covers the 15 member States of the Union plus Iceland, Norway and Liechtenstein.

What is Youth for Europe?

Education and vocational training are not the only opportunities for exchanges offered by the European Union. Outside school and work, this programme will enable you to meet other young people engaged on a common project, whether in the cultural, social or another field. It aims to offer young Europeans more opportunities to build a Europe that is closer to the citizen, where solidarity is more generally accepted and differences are respected.

Who can participate?

Youth organizations, local, regional, national or European organizations, government and non-governmental bodies engaged in youth affairs (e.g. voluntary service, training for organizers, information for young people, etc.) and young people themselves in the framework of youth measures.

The funds available
For 1995-99, ECU 126 million is allocated for the implementation of the programme.

Understanding the text

1. How do these programmes help to prepare young people for the European job market?
2. What types of people may participate in each of the programmes?

Going beyond the text

Choose one of the programmes you might want to participate in and write to the address printed above. Request information about the
– length of the programme,
– the costs,
– the countries involved,
– minimum age limit,
– the types of programmes on offer.

---

49 vocational training berufliche Ausbildung **52 placement** action of putting sb in a particular place **60 public bodies** group of people working as a unit for the public **63 to implement** ['ımplıment] to carry out; to put into practice **66 to adopt** to accept sth formally **92 voluntary service** freiwilliger Dienst (soziales Jahr) **95 framework** system

Merry Old England And Brave New Europe

Newspapers On The Internet

With the Internet you can always get hold of the latest news about Britain and Europe. Just by reading the headlines of various newspapers you can keep track of recent developments.

Daily Mail: http://www.dailymail.co.uk/
Daily Mirror: http://www.mirror.co.uk/
The Express/Daily Star: http://www.express.co.uk/
The Times: http://www.the-times.co.uk/
The Independent: http://www.independent.co.uk/
The European: http://www.the-european.com/
The Guardian: http://www.guardian.co.uk/
The Electronic Telegraph: http://www.telegraph.co.uk/
The Scotland Herald: http://www.theherald.co.uk/

Working with thematic vocabulary

Find 20 words in the texts of this chapter which have something to do with the relationship between Britain and Europe.

Our Environment: Don't Destroy It; Save It!

Don't Destroy It; Save It!

Getting to know our environment

1. Describe the pictures on page 122 and compare the three different types of environments.
2. What does the term "environment" mean to you?

Global Warming: The First Victims

Man is not the only animal threatened by global warming. The World Wide Fund for Nature says many plants and animals are already suffering the effects of pollution on the world's weather.

Diplomats discussing global warming in the air-conditioned UN headquarters in New York last week heard in a report for WWF in the United States that many of the world's national parks and other officially protected areas are already suffering from climate change. So, too, are some of the species that live in them.

"The giant pandas of Wolong in China, the grizzly bears of America's Yellowstone, and the tigers of India's Kanha National Park are among the animals at risk from global warming," said Adam Markham, director of the organisation's climate change campaign.

Man-made climate change – which most scientists now believe is being caused by the increasing emission of gases such as carbon dioxide from burning coal, oil, gas, wood and other fuels – is likely to affect different parts of the world in different ways.

But among those national parks, or protected areas thought to be particularly vulnerable, are the Coto Doñana in Spain, the Florida Everglades and the Moremi Game Reserve in Botswana, southern Africa.

Some animals are more vulnerable than others. If the climate changes gradually, many species can adapt or colonise new habitats, but some will be less lucky.

The giant panda, for example, is now restricted to comparatively small areas of Sichuan in south-western China. It survives in some of the world's richest areas of moist alpine and sub-alpine forests, themselves a product of the south-easterly monsoon winds. But climate forecasters believe global warming may change this. The panda is already under pressure from human use of land for farming and forestry. If habitat changes are too quick for it to adapt, it could become extinct.

Other animals that seem more adaptable could also lose out. The polar bear ranges widely and is an adept scavenger. But in its natural Arctic habitat it needs thick snow in which to build its dens, thick ice on which to roam and a steady supply of seals on which to feed. Arctic ice – and its food sources – are already retreating.

Farther from the Pole, the permafrost which underlies the northern tundra is also thawing, reducing range and food supplies for such animals as the reindeer. Some scientists predict 40 per cent of the world's tundra eco-systems may be lost by the end of the next century if global warming continues.

The Weekly Telegraph, July 10, 1997

---

1 to threaten *bedrohen* **3/4 to suffer** to experience sth unpleasant **4 effects** results **10 protected** kept safe **12 species** ['spiːʃiːz] class of plants or animals **21 emission** release or discharge of gas etc **carbon dioxide** [daɪˈɒksaɪd] *Kohlendioxyd* **23 fuel** material burned to produce heat or power **26 vulnerable** easily hurt or damaged **32 to colonise** to settle in and take control **habitat** natural environment of an animal or a plant **37 moist** slightly wet **39 monsoon** rainy season **44 extinct** no longer in existence **46 to range** to wander freely **47 adept** [-'-] expert, skilful **scavenger** animal that searches for decaying flesh as food **49 den** home of a wild animal **51 to retreat** here: to become smaller in size or extent **52 permafrost** soil that is permanently frozen deep beneath the earth's surface **53 to underlie** to exist under sth **tundra** large flat Arctic region of Europe, Asia and N America **to thaw** to become liquid or soft after being frozen **55 reindeer** *Rentier*

Internet World Wildlife Fund → http://www.wwf.org

Our Environment

ENDANGERED CREATURES

Reindeer
Loss of tundra eco-system, projected to reach 40%, will threaten habitat and food sources.

Grizzly bear
Scientists claim change in vegetation in South Alaska and N W British Columbia is causing loss of cover and food source for the bear.

Snow Finch
Retreating snow lines are reducing the habitat for this alpine bird.

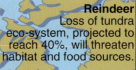

Monarch butterfly
Loss of moist air conditions is affecting the breeding and migratory patterns of this butterfly, endangering its survival.

Beluga Whale
Reduced krill stocks are affecting the food chain and bio-diversity of the oceans, threatening many whale species.

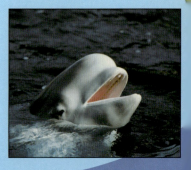

ATLANTIC OCEAN

EUROPE

SOUTH AMERICA

Don't Destroy It; Save It! **125**

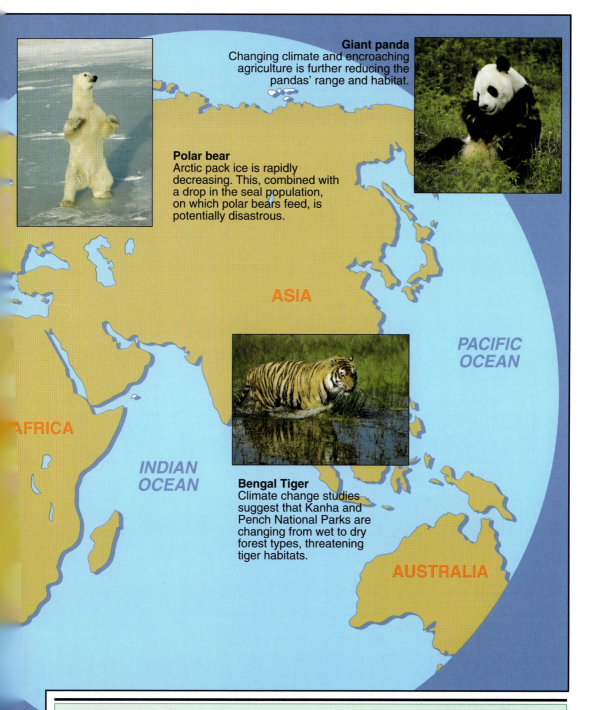

Giant panda
Changing climate and encroaching agriculture is further reducing the pandas' range and habitat.

Polar bear
Arctic pack ice is rapidly decreasing. This, combined with a drop in the seal population, on which polar bears feed, is potentially disastrous.

Bengal Tiger
Climate change studies suggest that Kanha and Pench National Parks are changing from wet to dry forest types, threatening tiger habitats.

---

endangered (adj) threatened with extinction **cover** place or area giving shelter or protection **krill** tiny sea creature **stock** supply or amount of sth available **diversity** variety, range **pack ice** large mass of ice floating in the sea **seal** *Seehund* **encroaching** (adj) *vordringend*

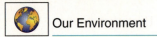

Our Environment

Understanding the text

1. What are the dangers of global warming according to the WWF report?
2. Explain the term "man-made climate change."
3. Why might the giant panda become extinct?
4. What are the natural habitats of the polar bear and the reindeer? How are these animals affected by global warming?

Working with the language

Go through the text and find one suitable noun for each of these verbs: threaten, protect, restrict, adapt, retreat, lose, endanger, disappear, reduce, encroach, decrease, change, decline.

Example: verb   noun
         to threaten   threat

Creative writing

Are these creatures worth saving? Express your views in a letter to a British newspaper. Support your argument with examples. Use vocabulary and information from the map and the article to help you.

An Ocean Of Concern

What's going into the seas and what's coming out?

Understanding the cartoon

1. What are the fish worried about?
2. How is marine life threatened?

Going beyond the cartoon

Comment on the general problem depicted in this cartoon.

---

concern worry **toxic** poisonous **doomed** certain to be destroyed **yep (infml)** yes

Don't Destroy It; Save It!

The Tracks We Left Behind Weren't Ours

Chevron is one of the world's leading oil companies. They explore and produce crude oil and natural gas in the United States and 21 other countries around the world.

The tracks we left behind weren't ours. Twelve years ago, we went to northwestern Montana in
5 search of oil. And there, in a remote corner of the Blackfeet Indian Reservation, we thought we'd find it. After all, hidden
10 under deposits of sandstone and shale lie countless dinosaur graves and, buried with them, the promise of petroleum.
15 But many steps had to be taken before we could even dig an exploratory well. First we reached an

A number of steps were taken to protect the grizzlies and their habitat: leaving the area to the bears in the spring by working only in the winter; exploring at an elevation far below grizzly dens; restricting human access; prohibiting off-road driving; installing a less obtrusive drill pad and revegetating the area.

agreement with the tribe over lease rights and royalty payments. We then hired an indepen-
20 dent environmental consultant who proposed a number of measures to protect the local grizzly bear population. All of which we adopted – from restricting human access to working straight through winter, then leaving, so the bears could forage undisturbed in the spring. Now did we actually discover oil there? No, we did not. But the process contributed to our creating in 1989 what remains one of the most envi-
25 ronmentally responsible policies in the industry. We call it Policy 530, and it is, quite candidly, a reality-based blend of smart business and genuine concern. True, it wasn't born out of pure altruism. But what it demands of us is the same. That we do what we need to do, then leave with hardly a trace.

People Do.

---

track trace **crude oil** *Rohöl* **6 remote** isolated **10 deposit** layer of matter, often deep under the earth, that has formed naturally **11 shale** *Schiefer* **11/12 countless** very many **17/18 exploratory well** *Probebohrloch* **19 lease rights** *Pachtrechte* **royalty payment** sum of money paid by the oil company to the owner of the land **20 consultant** sb who gives advice **21 to adopt** to accept **to restrict** to limit **access** ['ækses] right to use or enter sth **22 to forage** ['fɒrɪdʒ; US 'fɔːr-] to search or hunt for sth, esp food **24 to contribute to** to add to **25 policy** plan of action, statement of ideas **26 candid** open and honest **26 blend** mixture **smart** clever **genuine** ['dʒenjuɪn] honest **27 altruism** ['æltruɪzm] concern for the needs and feelings of other people above one's own

habitat natural environment of an animal or a plant **to explore** *erkunden* **elevation** level **den** home of a wild animal **to prohibit** to forbid **obtrusive** [-'--] disturbing **drill pad** *Bohrplattform* **to revegetate** *neu bepflanzen*

Understanding the text

1. Who is "we"?
2. What happened in northwestern Montana?
3. What is "Policy 530"?

Discussing the text

1. What type of text is this?
2. What image does Chevron want to present of itself?
3. Explain the usage of the words "track" and "trace" in the text.

Going beyond the text

Look for texts in newspapers and magazines which carry a similar message. Prepare a short presentation for class discussion.

Looking Forward To The Ride

Alex Trotman is the Chairman of the Ford Motor Company. This is a speech he delivered in Detroit, Michigan.

[…] Worldwide concern over the environment is accelerating. There are nearly 625 million cars and trucks in service around
5 the world today and in the next 30 years, the number of vehicles on the road is expected to reach one billion as markets open and living standards rise. That will
10 increase the concerns over crowded roads and increasing emissions. But at the same time, new customers will demand the rights to personal transportation
15 that have allowed individuals all over the world to pursue their personal goals and improve their standard of living. […]

The M25 is the motorway around London.

As for vehicles in the next century, I can't predict the future, but I do know they will be 20 lighter weight and very space efficient. They'll cool faster, use less power and offer greater fuel economy compared to the cars and trucks of today. They'll also 25 feature even more advanced electronics and computer technology that will make driving more efficient, easier, safer, more secure and cleaner. 30
At the same time we improve our cars and trucks, we're finding other ways to preserve the environment. Most people don't realize that in the United States, 35 vehicles are one of the most recycled durable consumer items. Seventy-five percent of the average car or truck produced or sold in the United States or Europe is now recy-

---

1 concern [kən'sɜːn] worry **2 to accelerate** to increase in speed **4 in service** in use **6 vehicle** ['viːəkl] machine (bus, car) for transporting goods, people etc. **12 emission** release or discharge of gas etc **16 to pursue** [-'-] to make an effort to achieve an aim or goal **26 to feature** to display or advertise sth **37 durable** ['---] likely to last for a long time

cled. Nearly 80 percent of both the Ford Contour and Ford Explorer, for example, can be recycled.

This ice scraper used to be a Ford Fiesta. It was made from Ford car bumpers collected from our dealers in Austria, Switzerland and Germany.

We've even made bird houses out of Broncos. We also use recycled consumer goods to make new vehicle parts. Fifty million recycled plastic soda bottles are used by Ford each year to make grille reinforcements, luggage racks and door padding. Old battery housings are made into splash shields and old bumpers into new bumper reinforcements. Used tires become brake pedal pads. [...]

To achieve the long-term solutions we'll need to make steady improvement in technology. This will happen faster and more effectively if industry, government and universities collaborate. [...]

Fortunately we have time to fashion the best solutions since no one suggests imminent danger or disaster as a result of climate change. But time mustn't be used as an excuse. The auto industry should be leaders in the push for a cleaner environment. That's our intention.

So that's what I wanted to tell you today. We aim to take the lead on new approaches that preserve the environment and keep customer priorities front and center. Innovative thinking, powered by advanced technology, fueled by consumer demand, driven by responsibility and common sense will take us there. Personally, I look forward to the ride.

Alex Trotman

Vital Speeches of the Day, December 1, 1996

Understanding the text

1. What reasons does Alex Trotman present for the increase in the number of vehicles on the road over the next thirty years?
2. How will vehicles in the future compare to those of today?
3. What steps does Trotman say Ford is taking to preserve the environment?

Analysing the text and the cartoons

1. Analyse the choice of vocabulary in the opening and closing statements of the speech.
2. Comment on the two cartoons.

Creative writing

In his speech, Alex Trotman refers to "concerns over crowded roads and increasing emissions." Prepare a list of suggestions to deal with these concerns.

---

43 ice scraper tool used for removing ice from a vehicle **44 bumper** bar fixed to the front and back of a vehicle to reduce the effect of an impact **50 grille** protective bars fixed to the front of a vehicle **reinforcement** [--'--] sth that is added to an object to make it stronger **51 padding** *Verkleidung* **housing** here: hard protective cover **52 splash shield** mudguard, the plastic piece behind the tyre which prevents dirt from the road from being splashed up onto the vehicle **53 tire** (Brit tyre) *Reifen* **58 to collaborate** [-'---] to work together **60 to fashion** to give form or shape to sth **61 imminent** ['---] about to happen

 Our Environment

Working with the language

1. Collect all the words and expressions belonging to the word-field "vehicle."
2. Put the first and second paragraphs (lines 1–30) into indirect speech. Start with: Alex Trotman said ...

Energy-Saving Tips For The Home

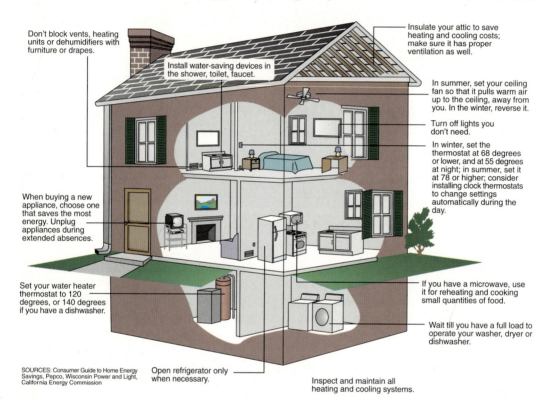

Don't block vents, heating units or dehumidifiers with furniture or drapes.

Install water-saving devices in the shower, toilet, faucet.

Insulate your attic to save heating and cooling costs; make sure it has proper ventilation as well.

In summer, set your ceiling fan so that it pulls warm air up to the ceiling, away from you. In the winter, reverse it.

Turn off lights you don't need.

In winter, set the thermostat at 68 degrees or lower, and at 55 degrees at night; in summer, set it at 78 or higher; consider installing clock thermostats to change settings automatically during the day.

When buying a new appliance, choose one that saves the most energy. Unplug appliances during extended absences.

Set your water heater thermostat to 120 degrees, or 140 degrees if you have a dishwasher.

If you have a microwave, use it for reheating and cooking small quantities of food.

Wait till you have a full load to operate your washer, dryer or dishwasher.

SOURCES: Consumer Guide to Home Energy Savings, Pepco, Wisconsin Power and Light, California Energy Commission

Open refrigerator only when necessary.

Inspect and maintain all heating and cooling systems.

Discussing the text

Compare your home to the one shown here in terms of energy-saving appliances and design features.

---

vent opening that allows air etc to pass out of or into a confined space **dehumidifier** [ˌdiːhjuːˈmɪdɪfaɪə(r)] *Luftentfeuchter* **drape** (Brit curtain) piece of material hung to cover a window **appliance** *Gerät* **to unplug** to take the plug *(Stecker)* out of the socket *(Steckdose)* **absence** the state of being away **faucet** (Brit tap) device for controlling the flow of water or gas out of a pipe or container **to insulate** to protect with a material to prevent loss of heat etc **load** amount

Internet Environmental Protection Agency → http://www.epa.gov

Don't Destroy It; Save It!

Dirty Harry

• TIME ENVIRONMENT CHALLENGE WINNER •

Dirty Harry

This is Harry. Harry is an average year-old European. In his first year, Harry has produced over 200 kg of waste, mostly diapers. But that's only the beginning. During his lifetime, Harry will produce over 650 tons of waste, garbage, toxic matter and other forms of pollution – single-handed! But he isn't unique. 650 tons is the average lifetime waste produced by every European. Harry and the rest of us can do a lot to stop this.

Let's stop using throw-away packaging! Let's hand back metal, glass and other valuable commodities for recycling. And let's stop buying cars which don't have catalytic emission control!
Will this help? You bet it will! It will reduce everyone's lifetime waste by over 150 tons. You'll be helping to save the environment. And making sure that Harry doesn't grow up to be Dirty Harry!

BSB/Adaptus, Stockholm

---

3 waste rubbish **diaper** [ˈdaɪəpə(r); US ˈdaɪpər] (Brit nappy) *Windel* **6 toxic** poisonous **7 single-handed** done by one person **8 unique** being the only one of its type **13 commodity** product, material **14/15 catalytic emission control** *Katalysator*

132  Our Environment

Understanding the text

1. What do we learn about Harry?
2. What can we do to prevent Harry from turning into "Dirty Harry"?

Going beyond the text

1. The environment is becoming swamped with waste. What measures have already been taken to solve this problem?
2. What other environmental problems are you aware of and what steps are being taken to try to solve them?

Working with the language

The following words are all synonyms for "waste": rubbish, garbage, refuse, trash, litter. Explain how these words differ in meaning and usage. Consult your dictionary for help.

Respect The Land

By treating our planet as a community, we can save our natural riches for future generations.

When we consider a subject as sweeping as the environment, we often focus on its most tangible aspects – the air we breathe, the water we drink, the food we put on the table. Those things are critically important. But to me the environment is also about something less tangible, though no less important. It is about our sense of community – the obligation we have to each other, and to future generations, to safeguard God's earth. It is about our sense of responsibility, and the realization that natural beauty and resources that took millions of years to develop could be damaged and depleted in a matter of decades.

Those are values I learned firsthand as a young boy on my family's farm in Carthage, Tennessee. We didn't call it environmentalism back then; it was simply common sense. My earliest environmental lessons came from our efforts to prevent soil erosion – by stopping the formation of gullies that would wash away the vital topsoil on which our farm depended. For a time, some large farmers who leased their land for short-term profits didn't worry about soil erosion: that's one of the reasons more than three hectares of prime topsoil floats past Memphis every hour, washed away for good.

As a teenager, I learned that such short-term thinking was causing even more serious problems. One of the books that we discussed around our family table was Rachel Carson's classic *Silent Spring* about pesticide abuse. As it did for millions around the world, Carson's book helped awaken in me an understanding that our planet's life is too precious to squander.

Today, the threats to our environment are even clearer to see – and much greater in scope and number. We live in a world where climate change, deforestation, holes in the ozone layer and air pollution are growing sources of concern. Our challenge is to find new ways to address those problems by reaching back to our oldest values of community and responsibility – by inspiring a greater respect for the land and the resources we share – even as economies and societies advance and develop around the world.

Fortunately, as I have raised a family of my own, I have learned that we have millions of powerful allies in this cause: our children. It is often children who remind their parents to recycle their cans, or to bundle their newspapers. It is often children who remind their parents of the simple miracles of nature – the crops that come from our farms, the parks and lakes and campsites where families and communities gather.

If we are to protect and preserve our environment on a global scale, we all must do our part, as nations, as families and as individuals. The need for awareness has never been greater, and the opportunity for us to make a difference is just as great. If we practice and teach the right kind of care and commitment for our environment, it will continue not only to bring us its natural gifts, but also to bring us together.

Al Gore

Time, October 27, 1997

---

1 subject topic or theme **sweeping** having a wide range or effect **2 to focus on sth** to direct attention, efforts, etc to a particular problem **2/3 tangible** [tændʒəbl] *greifbar, fühlbar* **7/8 sense of community** *Gemeinschaftsgefühl* **8 obligation** duty **9 to safeguard** to protect **11 realization** (Brit -isation) awareness **13 to deplete** to reduce greatly the quantity, size, etc of sth **a matter of** not more than **15 firsthand** coming directly from the original source **17 environmentalism** concern about the protection of the environment **20 soil** the upper layer of earth in which plants, trees, etc grow **21 gully** [ʌ] small valley or channel **vital** ['--] essential to the existence of sth **23 to lease** *pachten* **26 prime** most important **to float** to move in water **32 abuse** (n) [ə'bjuːs] wrong or excessive use of sth **35 precious** ['preʃəs] of great value **to squander** to waste foolishly or carelessly **37 scope** range or extent of sth **39 deforestation** *Abholzung* **42 to address** [-'-] to direct one's attention to sth, to deal with sth **46 to advance** to make progress **50 ally** ['ælaɪ] person, country, etc joined with another in order to give help and support **54 miracle** ['mɪrəkl] **crop** grain, fruit, etc collected from the fields **55 campsite** place for camping **57 to preserve** [-'-] to keep sth in its original state or in good condition **58 scale** scope, extent, range **63 commitment** willingness to give a lot of time, work, energy, etc to sth **65 gift** present

Our Environment

Understanding the text

1. What does the environment mean to Al Gore?
2. Which personal experiences from his youth awakened his interest in the environment?
3. What solutions to the most important environmental challenges does Al Gore suggest?
4. Who should take responsibility for preserving our environment?

Discussing the text

Comment on the subtitle "By treating our planet as a community, we can save our natural riches for future generations."

Going beyond the text

Explain how climate change, deforestation, holes in the ozone layer, and air pollution are interdependent.

Working with the language

Look for examples of the verb "to remind" in the text and explain the difference in usage.

Working with thematic vocabulary

Select the thematic vocabulary from the previous four texts and list the words according to the following categories:

soil depletion
waste
exploitation of resources
environmental protection
recycling

You may come across vocabulary which can be listed under several categories.

Acknowledgements

Illustrations

p. 7: Illustration by Steve Johnson and Lou Fancher, taken from: UTNE-Reader, September/October 1997, p. 87; p. 9: taken from: Sierra Club Engagement Calendar 1977. Photo: Robert Glenn Ketchum; p 13: Martin Laut; p. 19, 22: Emma Lou Marchant-Martin; p. 25: Rolf Krämer, Rösrath; p. 33 top: © Gert Wagner/Bilderberg; p. 33 bottom left: © Heilmann/laenderpress; p. 33 bottom right: Virginia Division of Tourism; p. 33 center: © MP/laenderpress; p. 36: Illustration by Joseph Fiedler, taken from: Emerge, February 1997, p. 53; p. 39: taken from: K.M. Kostyal: Compass American Guides: Virginia. Fodor's Travel Publications 1997, p. 239; p. 40: taken from: Booker T. Washington High School - Course Offerings and Descriptions; p. 42: © Gerry Gay/Tony Stone Images; p. 44: The Museum of the Confederacy; p. 46 top: Drawing by J. Karst, taken from: Trowbridge, A Picture of the Desolated States, Library of Congress 1868; p. 46 bottom: taken from: The American People: Creating a Nation and a Society. Ed. by Gary B. Nash, Julie Roy Jeffrey et al. New York: Harper & Row 1986, p. 548; p. 49: Photo: Ernest C. Whithers, taken from: Emerge, July/August 1997, p. 58; p. 50: Estate of Dr. Martin Luther King Jr.; p. 55, 56: Angelika Rösner/Verlagsarchiv Schöningh; p. 57: taken from: Frederic Ramsey, Jr.: Been here and Gone. New Brunswick: Rutgers University Press 1960, p. 169; p. 59: „All That Jazz" by Stuart White, USA; p. 60: Photo: Charles Walton IV, taken from: Southern Living, August 1991, p. 49; p. 61 top left, 61 bottom right, 61 center: Photo: Buddy Mays, taken from: Insight Guides: American Southwest. Ed. by Virginia Hopkins. Boston: APA Publications 1993; p. 61 bottom left: © Eberhard Grames/Bilderberg; p. 64: Photo: Donald Young, taken from: Insight Guides: American Southwest. Ed. by Virginia Hopkins. Boston: APA Publications 1993; p. 66 (2 photos): taken from: Explore the Navajo Nation, brochure; p. 68: © VVS/laenderpress; p. 69: Photo: Jerry Jacka, taken from: Arizona Highways, October 1981, p. 48; p. 70: © AP Photo/El Paso Times, Jack Kurtz; p. 71: © AP Photo/Lenny Ignelzi; p. 72: © dpa/Biggins; p. 73: Mexican American Cultural Center, San Antonio, Texas; p. 76 top left, 79: © dpa, Frankfurt; p. 76 top right: British Tourist Authority 1998; p. 76 bottom left: © Marion Schweitzer, München; p. 76 bottom right: © Copyright by Sportimage; p. 78: © Karen Robinson/FORMAT; p. 80: © Hayes Davidson, London; p. 82: Photo: Colin Cuthbert, taken from: Time, October 27, 1997, p. 38; p. 84: © Osprey Park, London; p. 86 (2 photos): Susan Ashworth-Fiedler/Verlagsarchiv Schöningh; p. 87: Scottsh Tourist Board 1995; p. 88: © British Telecommunications plc, 1998; p. 92: Tony Stone Images/Hulton Getty; p. 95, 97 left (2 cartoons): © Telegraph Group Limited, London, 1997; p. 98: Photo: David Gordon for Time, taken from: Time, October 27, 1997, p. 58; p. 101: © J.N. Hughes-Wilson; p. 104: taken from: This England, Winter 1997/98, p. 39; p. 105: taken from: New Statesman, January 2, 1998, p. 11; p. 108 top: © dpa/epa Archiv; p. 108 center left: © AP Photo/John Redman; p. 108 center right: © dpa/Gerry Penny EPA; p. 108 bottom: © AP Photo/John Redman; p. 109: Madeleine Waller; p. 111: The Weekly Telegraph, issue No. 337, 1997, p. 22; p. 113 (2 advertisements): Advertisement by Barry Delaney, taken from: New Statesman, January 2, 1998, p. 20 and 21; p. 115: taken from: This England, Winter 1997/98, p. 66; p. 116 top: PIB, Copenhagen; p. 116 bottom, 120: Mario Ramos; p. 117: © AP PHOTO/Roberto Pfeil; p. 118: taken from: New Statesman, January 2, 1998, p. 4; p. 122 top left: © The Image Bank/Benn Mitchell; p. 122 top right: Photo: Rick Careless, taken from: Beautiful British Columbia Magazine, Spring 1987, p. 6; p. 122 bottom: Mark Peterson - Saba; p. 124/125 (8 photos): © Reinhard-Tierfoto; p. 126: Illustration by Bateman; in: The Washington Post, December 8, 1997, p. 37; p. 127: © 1997 Chevron Corporation; p. 128: The Weekly Telegraph, February 28, 1997, issue No. 292, p. 6; p. 129: The Washington Post National/Weekly Edition, November 3, 1997, p. 28; p. 131: The advertisement was produced for the Time Environment Challenge by BSB/Adaptus, Stockholm, Sweden, photo by Marc Reto; p. 132: © Krömer/laenderpress

Texts

p.8: Eve Merriam, "How To Eat A Poem" from *Your Move* by Neil Fuller, Chequerboard, MacMillan Company of Australia, 1973, p. 22; **p. 9:** Anonymous, Matsuo Basho, "Haiku" from *The Teacher's and Writer's Handbook of Poetic Forms,* ed. by Ron Padgett New York, Teacher's and Writer's Collaborative, 1987, p. 89; **p. 10:** Tom Hawkins, "Wedding Night" from *Paper Crown* by Tom Hawkins, Ploughshares, Book Mark Press, 1989; **p. 12:** Barker Fairley, "Hunger" from *Canadian Poetry,* ed. by John R. Colombo, Edmonton, Hurtig Publishers, 1978, p. 94; **p. 13:** Barry Peters, "Arnie's Test Day" from *Sudden Fiction: 60 New Short-Short Stories,* ed. by Robert Shapard and James Thomas, New York, W.W. Norton & Co., 1996, pp. 240-242; **p. 16:** Vicki Feaver, "Coat" from *The Nation's Favourite Love Poems: A Selection of Romantic Verse,* ed. by

Acknowledgements

Daisy Goodwin, London, BBC Books, 1997, p. 130; **p. 17:** Wystan Hugh Auden, "Twelve Songs: IX" from *The Nation's Favourite Love Poems: A Selection of Romantic Verse,* ed. by Daisy Goodwin, London, BBC Books, 1997, p. 111; **p. 18:** Sherwood Anderson, "Discovery Of A Father" from *Memoirs of Sherwood Anderson,* ed. by Ray Lewis White, University of North Carolina Press, © 1939 by The Reader's Digest, © renewed 1966 by Eleanor Copenhaver Anderson. Abdruck mit Genehmigung der Liepmann AG, Zürich; **p. 23:** Elizabeth Bishop, "One Art" from *The Nation's Favourite Love Poems: A Selection of Romantic Verse,* ed. by Daisy Goodwin, London, BBC Books, 1997, p. 131; **p. 25:** William Inge, "The Tiny Closet" from *Summer, Brave and Eleven Short Plays,* Random House, 1962; **p. 37:** Don L. Lee, "The Primitive" from *The Black Poets,* ed. by Dudley Randall, Toronto, Bantam Books, 1971, p. 297; **p. 39:** Booker T. Washington, "Childhood In The Slave Quarters" from *Compass American Guides: Virginia* by K.M. Kostyal, Fodor, 1997, pp. 238-239; **p. 43:** Robert P. Broadwater, "The Spy's A Broad" from *Daughters of the Cause* by Robert P. Broadwater, ed. by Joseph T. Campbell, Martinsburg, Daisy Publishing, pp. 25-28; **p. 45:** "Reconstruction: Rebuilding The South" from *USIA information sheet,* written by Jonathan Rose, 1986; **p. 51:** Son Seals, "Going Back Home" from *The Lost Roads Project: A Walk-in-book of Arkansas* by C.D. Wright, Fayetteville, University of Arkansas Press, 1994, p. 32; **p. 52:** Mildred D. Taylor, "You Stand Accused Of Being Black" from *Let the Circle Be Unbroken* by Mildred D. Taylor, Dail Books for Young Readers, Penguin Books, 1981; **p. 56:** "River Riddles" from *English Teaching Forum,* Vol. XXIX, No. 1, January 1991; **p. 57:** "Singing These Old Lonesome Blues" from *Long Journey Home* by Julius Lester, Penguin 1991; **p. 58:** "Jazz And Jazzmen" from *English Teaching Forum,* Vol. XXIX, No. 1, January 1991; **p. 60:** "Iced Tea: The Champagne Of The South" from *USA Cookbook* by Sheila Lunkins, New York, Workman Publishers, 1997; **p. 62:** "Endless Horizons" from *Insight Guides - American Southwest,* ed. by Virginia Hopkins, Third Edition, Massachusetts, Houghton Mifflin Company, 1993, p. 77; **p. 63:** "The People Of The Southwest: Their Past And Present" from *Lonely Planet Travel Survival Kit: Southwest USA* by Rob Rachowiecki, Hawthorn (Australia), Lonely Planet Publications 1995, p. 11 and 12; **p. 65:** "Explore The Navajo Nation" from *Explore The Navajo Nation,* brochure by Navajoland Tourism Department, Arizona; **p. 67:** "Navajo Nation Parks Rules & Regulations" from *Discover Navajoland, Visitor's Guide,* brochure by Navajoland Tourism Department, Arizona; **p. 68:** "What Time Is It?" from *Canyon Overlook Guide, A Visitor's Guide to Canyon De Chelly National Monument,* brochure by Navajoland Tourism Department, Arizona; **p. 69:** Diane Glancy, "Without Title" from *English Teaching Forum,* July 1994; **p. 71:** William Booth, "Hot On The Trail" from *The Washington Post National Weekly Edition,* September 1, 1997, p. 9; **p. 73:** "Along The Rio Grande" from *The Economist,* December 12, 1992; **p. 73:** "San Antonia Facts" from *San Antonio Facts,* brochure by The Greater San Antonio Chamber of Commerce, San Antonio; **p. 74:** "So Long 'Dallas', Hello High Tech" from *Newsweek,* April 21, 1997, p. 34; **p. 77:** "Statistics" from: Britain In Numbers by Mairi Ben Brahim, *Time,* October 27, 1997, p. 37; **p. 77:** "'Rich South, Poor North' - Tell That To The Cornish" from: Cornwall, County on the Edge, *The Economist,* March 7, 1998, p. 46; **p. 79:** "The Millennium Dome" from: Inside the Dome: Millennium Wonders are Unveiled, *The Weekly Telegraph,* March 4, 1998; **p. 82:** "Britain's Cities Are Booming" from: The Music of the Metropolis, *The Economist,* September 27, 1997, p. 44; **p. 84:** "Business success..." from *CNT-Advert;* **p. 85:** Kathleen Morgan, "Scotland's Cultural Cocktail" from *As It Happens, Scotland. When Will You Go?,* brochure by Scottish Tourist Board, 1995; **p. 88:** "A Vision Of The Highlands" from *BT-Advert;* **p. 89:** Geddes Thomson, "Pride Of Lions" from *Streets of Stone,* Edinburgh, The Salamander Press, 1985; **p. 92:** Judy Goodkin, "Hometown" from: Hometown Bernice Rubens, *The Times Magazine,* August 23, 1997, p. 42; **p. 95:** "Decisive Vote By Scots" from *The Weekly Telegraph,* October 8, 1997, p. 24; **p. 97:** "The Welsh Decision" from: Wales Winning the Peace, *The Economist,* September 27, 1997, p. 48; **p. 98:** Michael Ignatieff, "A United Kingdom?" from: A Gamble with History, *Time,* October 27, 1997, p. 58; **p. 102:** Stephen Bates, "English Is The Most Commonly Taught Language In Europe" from *The Guardian Weekly,* February 22, 1998; **p. 103:** Roger Dykes, "The Madness Of Metrication" from *This England,* Winter 1997, p. 38; **p. 104:** Margaret Walker, "Measure For Measure" from *This England,* Winter 1997, p. 39; **p. 107:** David Ward, "Farmers Philosophical Over Latest Blow" from *The Guardian Weekly,* August 18, 1996, p. 24; **p. 109:** Bill Jamieson, Sir Roy Denman, "Would It Have Been Better If We Hadn't Joined The EU?" from *The Weekly Telegraph,* No. 337, 1997; **p. 114:** Robin Cook, "A Modern Britain, With America And In Europe" from *International Herald Tribune,* May 21, 1997; **p. 115:** "Hilaire Belloc's View" from *The Cruise of the "Nona",* 1925; **p. 116:** "An Interview With Britain's Prime Minister" from *Time,* October 27, 1997, p. 44; **p. 118:** "Education And Training: Tackling Unemployment In The European Market" from *Office For Official Publications of the European Communities,* Luxembourg; **p. 123:** "Global Warming: The First Victims" from: The World's 10 Most Endangered Creatures, *The Weekly Telegraph,* July 10, 1997, p. 14; **p. 127:** "The Tracks We Left Behind Weren't Ours" from *Chevron-Advert;*

Acknowledgements

p. 128: Alex Trotman, "Looking Forward To The Ride" from: The Environment And How to Preserve It, *Vital Speeches of the Day,* December 1, 1996, pp. 121-123; **p. 130:** John Anderson, "Energy-Saving Tips For The Home" from *The Washington Post National Weekly Edition,* December 8, 1997, p. 10; **p. 131:** "Dirty Harry" from *Time,* 1991, text and photo by BSB/Adaptus, Stockholm; **p. 132:** Al Gore, "Respect The Land" from *Time, Special Issue,* Supplement to the Time Magazine, October 27, 1997, pp. 8-9.

Every effort has been made to supply complete copyright information for the texts and pictures included here. Should such entries be incomplete or contain errors, we request copyright owners to contact the publishers so that we can proceed with the necessary corrections and/or customary compensation.